Brick

a literary journal

number 65/66

fall 2000

ISSN 0382-8565

ISBN 0-968755-0-X

Publications Mail Agreement # 1756346

EDITOR: Linda Spalding

CONTRIBUTING AND MANAGING EDITOR: Michael Redhill

CONTRIBUTING EDITORS: Michael Ondaatje, Esta Spalding

ASSISTANT EDITOR: Emmet Mellow

OMBUDSPERSON: Cecily Môos

We gratefully acknowledge the support of
The Canada Council and the Ontario Arts Council

Brick accepts unsolicted manuscripts of non-fiction *only*.
Please send submissions with appropriate return postage to:

BRICK

Box 537, Stn Q

Toronto, Ontario

M4T 2M5 Canada

Submissions may also be e-mailed to mredhill@interlog.com

Subscribe on-line! WWW.BRICKMAG.COM

BRICK is published twice yearly and is printed and bound
in Canada by Transcontinental Printing
Distributed in the United States by Publishers Group West

In This Issue

Also in this issue: cartoons by Margaret Atwood and the rediscovered photographs of Jacqueline Rau

Cover painting by Yves Berger. Cover designed by Rick/Simon. Brick logo by David Bolduc.

Welcome Errata

by Cecily Möos (Mrs.)

IT IS WITH GREAT PLEASURE and with boundless regret that I welcome you to and apologize for *Brick, a Literary Journal.*

But let me first accentuate the positive. I have been invited by the publisher of this now-stout organ to speak on behalf of the entire staff in welcoming you to this, the beginning of a new era for the magazine. The changes you find within and without are a result of a lengthy congress held in the magazine's headquarters concerning its future. (These deliberations were of a nature too technical to be intelligible to our readership, but those who wish to know more may send away for the minutes, collected in a sister publication entitled *More Readers, More Money: How?*)

Suffice it to say the magazine you now hold in your hands is the fruit of these soul-searching talks. It is larger. It is easier on the eye. It has cartoons. Also, you may well have paid American dollars for it. Lest our readers in Moncton fear this a sign of renewed Fenian raids, let me reassure them that it is simply a result of *Brick* now being dispensed to American readers on their own soil. This is due to a new distributor chosen for its innocence concerning exchange rates. What this portends for Canadian readers is not much, except that it will certainly be the occasion of a welcome decline in cross-border shopping.

As for content, the new *Brick* resembles the old inasmuch as it is energized by the same editorial thrust. But the new *Brick* will also be responsive to the will of our readers. For instance, to those of our correspondents who have complained of late that *Brick* no longer runs lengthy essays about colonic irrigation, I direct them immediately to page 80 of this issue where they will find the situation ably remedied.

In summation, it is with great pride that I welcome you, on behalf of our entire establishment, to this grand new chapter in *Brick*'s history. If you do not each and every one of you buy a subscription, we shall be dead in three months.

THIS NOW BRINGS ME to a slightly less cheerful task. In my capacity of Chief Apologist for the magazine, it falls to me to express the heartfelt horror we all feel as a result of the innumerable errors and oversights which somehow creep past our proofreading departments. With extreme regret, I must ask readers who are in possession of our previous number to get it now. I will wait. Please turn to page 79 of that most distasteful example of our stock in trade, and there you will find a photo of the hardworking staff of this journal, and below it, a roster of who is there pictured. In that list, due to some opprobrious breach of protocol, the correct order of the names E. Mëllow and E. Spälding have been reversed. My deepest apologies to both members of our staff and any readers whose letters were misdirected as a result.

Next, I offer a tearful apology to Kenneth Sherman, whose contributor note in our last issue credited him with a poem he is not the author of. The said work, entitled *Life, A Poem*, does not exist, which spares us at least the unpleasant task of apologizing to the real author. However, should anyone compose a poem with the above title at any point in the future, I hope he or she will accept in advance our most earnest expressions of remorse for attributing their masterwork to someone else. Someone who, I might add, did not seem the least bit grateful for the honour.

Finally, in our previous issue, for やがてまぎるる , please read わが身ともがな .

AS A LAST WORD, I would like our readers to know that this issue of Brick marks a milestone of another sort. For it is with this number that an embarassing chapter in the magazine's history comes to an end. To wit: this is the first issue in three that we have not inflicted some form of injury on Ms. Gunda Lambton of Alcove, Quebec, with the exception, of course, of this sentence, for which I know our entire staff joins me in expressing the deepest contrition.

Welcomingly and apologetically yours,

Cecily Möos

In my Toronto suburb

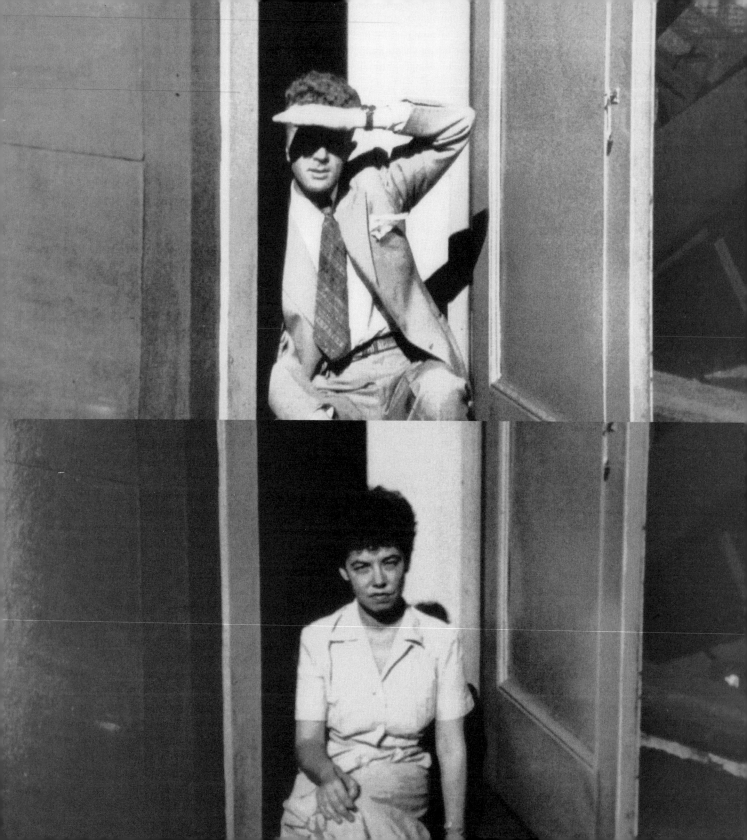

Finding Paul Bowles

JENNIFER BAICHWAL

P: *It's impossible, of course, to recreate truth in words. It's not possible.*
   But then . . . truth can only be expressed in words. (long pause)
J: *That's a bit of a dilemma.*
P: (laughs) *Well, that's all right. If it wants to be a dilemma, I don't mind.*

FROM 1994 to 1998 I made a film about Paul Bowles called *Let It Come Down*. I was preoccupied with the problem of biography. And whether it was that preoccupation which brought me to Paul Bowles or Paul Bowles who created the preoccupation, I still am not sure. The two ideas—Bowles, biography—have become so mixed up in the past years that thinking about one always eventually leads back to the other.

I first met Bowles in 1984, at the age of twenty. I had run away to Morocco—it was his prose which led me there—to escape university and my family. The country was intoxicating, and I ended up staying a year, living on a farm outside the town of Asilah.

When I arrived in Tangier, I made the pilgrimage to Bowles' door, awkward and intimidated. The man who ushered me in and then lounged, cat-like, against cushions in a dark corner was gracious, elegant, and remote. The room was heavy with carpets and the odour of kif, which Bowles smoked with the help of a long black cigarette holder. The scene sounds exotic, but the fact was that Bowles was not exotic at all. He could more easily have been imagined in a dozen other settings—a London drawing room, a New York club—than North Africa.

Americans rarely achieve the exotic anyway: the culture's open-faced enthusiasm precludes it. But Bowles was not that. He was opaque and impermeable. He had an appearance which seemed fixed, unaffected by circumstance. Someone described him in the desert, which brings out the dishevelled in everyone, as the quintessential New England gentleman, dressed in a perfectly pressed suit and tie. I knew, from his books, that there was something seething underneath. But it was submerged enough to leave no trace on the surface.

I STARTED reading Bowles as a teenager. I began with *The Collected Stories* and I still think the stories are the best introduction to his work (rather than the default favourite, *The Sheltering Sky*). He has a gift for the macabre—it is no coincidence that his mother used to read him Poe—but a macabre which is lean, almost laconic. I remember being drawn to the impartial quality of his prose, his ability to erase himself in it. Bowles writes with such economy of gesture, yet is able to convey an entire interior landscape through one descriptive sentence. We learn more from the facial spasm, the raised voice, the "smell of whiskey that had been drunk and whiskey that had been spilled," than what pages of trying to plunge inside the character would convey. There is the voyeur's meticulous observation in Bowles, and nothing given is arbitrary. As he once wrote to David McDowell:

No one seems to have realized that practically all the tales are a variety of detective story. Not the usual variety, I admit, but still, detective stories in which the reader is the detective; the mystery is the motivation for the characters' behaviour, and the clues are given in the form of reactions on the part of the characters to details of situation and surroundings. If Chalia moves her bed out from the wall each night before she goes to bed, there is a reason for it. If Van says, "Gee I was burned up last Friday," if Bouchta's eyes in Mokhtar's dream remind him of the eyes in the head of a roasted sheep at Aïd el Kébir, if the employee on the river boat has a "somewhat simian" face and the husband walks toward him offering to pay the supplementary fare to him and then "remembers" that his wife has his wallet, there is a reason, and it is usually the reason for the entire story. Often the action of a story is predicated on a bit of unmentioned, subconscious knowledge on the part of a protagonist, but the suggestion is always made and placed in an emotional frame which serves as a clue to anyone who really read the story.

It is a kind of democracy with the reader—a generosity, a collaborative act. He tells you only as much as you need to know and then lets you find the rest. There is a lovely passage in Gore Vidal's introduction to the *Collected Stories* about one of them:

I was surprised to note how the actual stories differ from my memory of them. I recalled a graphic description of a sixteen-year old boy's seduction of his father on a hot summer night in Jamaica. Over the years, carnal details had built up in my memory like a coral reef. Yet on re-reading "Pages From Cold Point," nothing (and everything) happens. In his memoirs, Bowles refers, rather casually, to this story as something he wrote aboard ship from New York to Casablanca: "a long story about a hedonist . . ." It is a good deal more than that.

Bowles, when I reminded him of the passage, explained his approach:

The son saw to it that he had sex with his father in order to blackmail him. But it's scarcely noticeable in the telling of the story. He just suggests that they invite Uncle Charles down. And the father says, "There's no room for him." The son says, "In my room, it's empty." That's all there is. It was supposed to make the reader believe in all kinds of things which were not mentioned. Why would one mention it? Especially if the reader's imagination can do it so much better.

For a number of years, Bowles was one of those writers with a particular, fervent following who remained more or less unknown to the mainstream reader. Bertolucci's film of *The Sheltering Sky* changed that somewhat, but there was still something persistently marginal about him. Vidal in the same introduction talks about Bowles expatriating himself, and how that prevented him from receiving more acclaim in the United States:

As a short story writer, he has had few equals in the second half of the twentieth century. Obvious question: If he is so good, why is he so little known? Great American writers are supposed not only to live in the greatest country in the world (the United States, for those who came in late), but to write about that greatest of all human themes: *The American Experience*. From the beginning of the Republic, this crude America First-ism has flourished. . . . Paul Bowles has lived most of his life in Morocco. He seldom writes about the United States.

I asked Bowles about his relationship with the U.S.:

J: Do you remember when *The Time of Friendship* came out and there was a critic, John Grey, who said "Bowles has not adopted his style to the changing years, with the result that he now seems old-fashioned. It's not a question of a lack of contemporary facts, but of a basic disharmony with the prevailing gist. This is always a problem with the expatriate writer, as has been evidenced by Lawrence Durrell, and Bowles' problem seems to be focused on an inability to deal simultaneously with two cultures."

P: What would the two cultures be?

J: Morocco and America, I guess.

P: But I wasn't dealing with America at all.

J: That's the point. I guess he thought that because you were an American writer, your perspective was American by default.

P: Why would he assume that?

J: Because that's where you were born and that's the context you grew up in.

P: Uh-huh. Until I rejected it. Once you reject something, it doesn't bother you any more.

J: Did you completely reject American society?

P: Yes, I think I did.

J: Why?

P: Oh, I'd had enough of it. I didn't agree with, I suppose, the fundamentals in America. I still don't. I think it's a terrible country. I wouldn't want to live there again.

J: What kind of fundamentals do you mean?

P: Well, the emphasis on success. That seems to me a very vicious element in any society. What one needs is enough to eat and a place to live, but one can generally provide that somehow without success. But I know Americans want big success. Gore himself. He always said, "I want a red carpet between the plane and my hotel." Yes, but very seriously he said it. I remember we were at Christopher Isherwood's in

Santa Monica, and I began to laugh. And Gore said "Oh! I mean it!" You know: he didn't mean it but he did mean it. That's what he would have liked.

Instead of adopting the heroic individualism of expatriate writers like Hemingway, Bowles seemed to be completely devoid of self-consciously American characteristics. This is not to say that he was a chameleon who took on the qualities of the various cultures he encountered. Rather, he retained, everywhere, the singularity of a stranger. To what extent this deliberate marginality was based on colonial exploitation (of which Bowles' wealthy friends, who lived in mansions with servants, were much more visible examples), is a murky question.

J: Do you think it's somehow irresponsible to live in another culture without participating in it?

P: No, why? I think one has the right to live wherever any government will allow one to live. And one really should have the right to live anywhere on the surface of the planet. And participating in the idiosyncrasies of the individuals who live there seems to me almost foolish to try. Why would one imitate the natives, wherever one went? One is oneself—you don't have to imitate anybody or any social tradition. I can imagine that there could be a debate on the subject. Because the other side would say, "But human beings are human beings and should really have some kind of contact with other human beings." Well, that's their idea, that's fine. Mine is what it says in *The Thousand and One Nights*. "I can think of no greater delight than to be a foreigner, among those who are not of my kind."

AS MY MOROCCO YEAR progressed, I became more embroiled in the intrigues and vicissitudes of village life and only saw Bowles a few more times. He would ask for, and relish, descriptions of my entanglements. The visits ended abruptly when the writer Mohammed Mrabet, who was often around in those days, threatened to split my Moroccan boyfriend's head open with a hammer. We retreated, and I left the country a few weeks afterwards.

I kept up with Bowles' work in the intervening years but as his writing trailed off, so did my attention. Then in 1994, ten years after our first meeting, I woke up in the middle of the night after a dream in which someone, who had just been to Tangier, told me that Bowles had died. In the insommnial and oddly sombre hours which followed, I calculated his age—eighty-three—and reflected on the lack of an authentic likeness or record.

I wrote to him then about making a film, he cautiously replied, and thus began a four year odyssey during which I spent more time thinking about another individual than I imagined was possible, slid into horrendous debt (because the film is self-financed), met my husband Nick de Pencier (who is the cinematographer and producer) and found myself witnessing the passing of a literary generation. We went to Morocco in 1994 and again in 1996 where I conducted a marathon interview with Bowles over ten days, which forms the basis of the film. In between, we visited Kansas to talk to William Burroughs and went to New York in the fall of 1995 because Bowles travelled there—his first trip to the city in thirty years—for a festival of his music at Lincoln Center.

In New York, we recorded what turned out to be a final meeting. Bowles had invited Burroughs from Kansas to lunch at his hotel and Burroughs unexpectedly brought Allen Ginsberg with him. The lunch was hilarious: three old men reminiscing about trying to quit smoking, complaining about their sandwiches, gossiping about all the drugs (now prescription) their friends were taking. At one point, they get into a heated discussion about the existence of God:

Ginsberg: I apparently asked Jane [Bowles] a question once that displeased her or shocked her.

Bowles: Hmm?

Ginsberg: Or startled her . . .

Burroughs: I'll tell you what you said!

Ginsberg: I *remember* what I said. I asked her whether she believed in God.

Burroughs (*imitating Ginsberg*): "Do you believe in God, Jane?"

Bowles: Oh, that!

Ginsberg: We were shopping on Boulevard Pasteur and we were engaging in small talk. I was a little wobbly at the time on my theistic versus non-theistic views. I asked her, thinking that she had had some kind of visionary experience that was serious. So, I was interested. I don't know what her reaction was, but I think in a letter I read that she thought this was an impertinent question.

Bowles: In her letter to me, she said that you asked her that on the telephone.

Burroughs: That's what I heard.

Ginsberg: No!

Bowles: And she said—

Bowles and Burroughs in unison: I'm certainly not going to discuss it on the telephone! (*They both laugh heartily.*)

Ginsberg: No, no! I remember very clearly—

Burroughs: Well, that's what I heard.

Ginsberg: —My recollection is on Boulevard Pasteur when she was shopping with a shopping bag!

Bowles: No, no.

Ginsberg: It's a Rashomon situation then.

Burroughs: Did Jane believe in God?

Ginsberg: Oh, she didn't give me an answer. I think she said, "What a question!"

Burroughs: *I* believe in God.

Ginsberg: Since when?

Burroughs: Always! I always have.

Ginsberg: A closet theist, all along.

Burroughs (*shrugs*): Anybody who reads my books would realize that.

Ginsberg to Bowles: And you? Do you believe in God? Now that we have the question on the table.

Bowles (*throws his head back and laughs*): Never did, no. My family didn't teach me to, when I was a child. Because they didn't believe. But they told me I must never make fun of people who do. So I never have ridiculed *les croyants*.

BIOGRAPHY IS HAZARDOUS. Trying to sum up the innumerable particularities, contradictions and experiences which comprise another individual seems often to end in failure. There is one extreme of using overweening psychological interpretation (he hated his father) as an organizing filter. There is another of assuming that recitation of chronological fact can stand in as the record of a life. I wanted to find an alternative—rather, I was forced to find an alternative—because I knew Bowles to be a character singularly unsuitable for traditional biography.

There had been some significant efforts over the years: profiles, documentaries, interviews, a book. But he never came across. In fact, all his efforts on these occasions were directed entirely towards obfuscation. There is a deep evasion at his center which consistently resists the assimilation of all

that he has experienced, written or composed. He even managed to preserve anonymity in his own autobiography, *Without Stopping*. There is an exchange in the film between Bowles and William Burroughs on the subject:

Bowles: Burroughs didn't like my autobiography. He called it *Without Telling*. That was his idea of a proper title. I never understood why.

Burroughs: Well, because it didn't tell anything! This memoir of Gore Vidal [*Palimpsest*]—very

. . . very entertaining—it's just come out. Very good. There's some little scandalous story on every page! None in Paul. Nothing about his own sex life, *nothing*.

Bowles: Yes, but . . . one may feel something without telling what one feels. And certainly it's not proper to tell what you feel. At least I was always taught that.

Burroughs: That's very "New England." And he is very "New England" in many ways.

Where others leave clues—the prescription bottles in the bathroom, the half-finished love letter underneath others on the desk, the extravagant alcohol-induced eruption—Bowles (a teetotaller, by the way) denied any essential connection between the world and himself. He stoically endured the erosion of physical privacy which accompanies old age, but resisted, flat out, any tendency towards the garrulous. He remained deliberately (and maddeningly) enigmatic:

P: How can one talk about oneself intelligently? I can't. I wouldn't know what to say. And you say what is my idea of myself? Somebody who wrote a few stories and wrote a little music and then went on and probably dropped dead. It's not very important what he did.

I'm extremely aware of the vast difference between how other people see me and how I see myself. That which is seen from without is bound to distort that which is seen from within. And I can't imagine how I strike other people. Not knowing that, I can't very well make a comparison and a contrast with what I think about myself. It's very hard. I don't think about myself at all, and I don't think I have any particular qualities that distinguish me from someone else, so there's not much to say or to think.

J: Do you think anyone really knows you?

P: Knows me? No . . . I don't think anybody knows anyone. I think people are planets floating. Spheres. So if they touch, they just touch at one tiny point. That's the maximum touching. But I think in general they don't touch at all, they just float around. Self-sufficient.

WHEN WE TRAVELLED to Morocco in 1994, Bowles was cordial and funny but as opaque as ever. There was a collection of anecdotes he'd tell over and over again—stock tales about Morocco and his famous friends—all of which I had heard before in one form or another. When he invited us back in 1996, I wanted to break past that point, and devised all kinds of elaborate strategies to achieve this. In the end, they proved unnecessary: he simply chose to reveal himself. That may be because he was at the end of his life and already in a state of almost continual reflection. It gave him an air of the omniscient: fully neither in life nor death, he spent his days surveying both from some lofty interim vantage point.

P: Meaning is a human thing, isn't it? Yes. You can't speak of a tree as having a meaning or a rock as having a meaning. But people love to speak of the process of life as having a meaning. That is a religious concept really—comes from it. It's an outcropping of a belief in supernatural powers. Obviously, for every individual, life has a meaning. There's as many meanings as there are people. But life in total has no meaning whatever.

J: Are you admitting that there is meaning in your life?

P: I'm admitting that there are some things I want, certain things I get. And that's part of meaning in life, yes. But it's not important. If one lives or dies, there's no meaning either way. And one always does die. Whatever is alive has to die. Well, maybe that's the meaning of life. The meaning of life is inevitable death.

The intimacy which results in the biographer/subject relationship is unlike any other. First there is the utterly disproportionate familiarity which comes from spending all that time thinking about, reading about, writing about or listening to, someone else. You end up knowing a lot about that person, and in the case of Bowles, he seemed to take it for granted after a while that I was there for all of his life, observing whatever happened. The familiarity breeds power, which if the biographer is not sympathetic to the subject, can be ugly and destructive. On the other hand, for sympathy to become hagiography is failure. Having tried and rejected all the conventional ways of telling his life story, editing the film simply became about finding Bowles: by the end of it, I wanted you to feel as though you had spent some time with him.

I took *Let It Come Down* to Bowles in November 1998, just under a year before he died. He had not seen me since 1996, although I occasionally wrote to him about the film's progress, or lack of it. All through the editing process, where I spent hundreds of hours with the virtual Bowles and none with the actual, I was afraid that he would die before I could show the film to him. Then, when I was nearly finished, I was afraid of the opposite: that he would still be alive, so I would have to let him see it. Would an adverse reaction make the film unsuccessful to me? Was an adverse reaction inevitable? I had just returned from India, where I was shooting another documentary in which I had, far too casually, made a subject of myself. The film is about me and my siblings taking my father's ashes back to India, where he was born, to disperse them at the source of the Ganges river. In it, I had become biographer and subject simultaneously and the two selves were constantly at each other's throats. The experience made me more aware of the perils, in Bowles' mind, of his exposure.

I had spent a good deal of time in India comparing it to Morocco. Because I was in some complicated way *of* India, I could not lose myself there, I felt responsible for it. Morocco, on the other hand, had always been inexhaustible in its mystery. Back in Tangier, the place I had spent so much time trying to look at through Bowles' eyes, I was filled with apprehension, but it was muted by inevitability. The old, rushing feeling, the ache from some visceral memory of the place, which always choked me up when I arrived, hadn't come at the airport. But sitting on the balcony of the hotel with a glass of mint tea, looking out over the medina, with the evening call to prayer reverberating all around me—somehow, I felt comfortable because the foreignness was impenetrable. And this, I finally realized, was Bowles' reason for staying so long: when you belong nowhere then you belong, eventually, to that. And that was at least one reason for my affinity with him.

When I arrived at his apartment, Rodrigo Rey Rosa was there visiting. Bowles was eighty-seven then, nearly blind from glaucoma and mostly bedridden. He had emphysema, which means that he wasn't smoking as much kif as he used to. But he was still as sharp as a tack. Despite my initial strenuous protests, Bowles insisted on watching the film that evening. I had intended to give it to him, leave, and have him write to me after he watched it. I was prepared for him to despise it, as he had rejected almost everything else that has been produced about him over the years. I wanted, however, to avoid having him despise it to my face.

In the face of his polite requests, I realized that it was churlish and selfish to continue to demure. After all, it was more of a risk for him to watch it

than for me to witness his reaction. So I set him up two inches from the set (which is in his bedroom), adjusted the volume, closed the door and went to sweat it out in the living room. I picked up a volume edited by Daniel Halpern on the writer's identity. *Borges and I* was included and I read it, over and over again, for seventy-five minutes. I could hear everything: the film's soundtrack was punctuated by Bowles' comments as well as his silences. Sometimes the comments were funny: "Oh, Bill's here! Nice to see him!" as though Burroughs were there in the room with him. Or: "What's he (meaning himself, onscreen) doing now?" Sometimes they were sharp: "Who said that? What a windbag!" after a particularly pointed comment from Mohammed Choukri or David Herbert. The silences were always ominous.

As the film drew to a close, I went to hide in the kitchen, wondering if I should escape and put off the moment of reckoning. Rodrigo found me there, sheepish in hesitation. It should not have been a surprise to me that Bowles was able to remove himself from himself enough to be polite in his reaction. But he was more than polite—he was effusive, and that was a relief.

AN IRONY of the biographer/subject relationship is that what appears to be a beginning for one is an ending for the other. For Bowles, after 1996, I became a memory, brought back to life through infrequent correspondence. I, on the other hand, was with him every day, all day, busy trying to explore the remotest corners of his psyche. Now, after seeing the film, he had accepted the intimacy I required in order to find him during all those months in the edit room. The film was a compressed record of the search for his likeness; because it had some truth, because I had shown that in some way I *knew* him, I had won him over. It was a confirmation of rapport. But I, I realized only after arriving there, was in Tangier seeking resolution. I had come to say goodbye. For me, making the film was a search to explain to myself my twenty-year fascination with Bowles. The completed film had *become* the explanation, and there was no obvious question left to be answered by further experience.

As I walked aimlessly for hours through Tangier's tortuous alleys, which now no longer seemed as exotic, I was in turmoil at the finality of it. Was this the biographer's revenge for spending all that time with the other, a *Pale Fire*-like revolution in which the commentator looms ever larger and the subject finally becomes insignificant, rejected? Or was it that four years with someone was enough; that I, having completed the task, was legitimately claiming back my attention for something else?

I still don't know the answer to that question. Bowles' death last year closed the matter in another way, and I now regret that I did not return once more for a purely social visit: to be with, rather than record. But then, as I sat with Bowles in his tiny, cluttered bedroom for the last time, it was clear that what we had in common was everything about him and his life. And this, I was astonished to discover, did not seem to be enough to sustain us as friends.

from

The page-turner's sister

JEAN MCKAY

Echo

We spent a month at a cottage on a little lake in Muskoka. I'd say I was fifteen, on the basis of my emotional maturity, and what from this vantage point I think fifteen means, but I must have been nineteen because I knew who Spinoza was. Well, twenty; Spinoza was second year Philosophy, not first. OK, I was twenty. I spent a lot of time floating in a canoe, looking down into the water as the sun struck through suspended particles of dirt, and thinking about Spinoza's motes.

There was an echo on that lake, if you found the right spot, that would give you a delay, and then come back very precisely. A large enough delay so that I could play eight running sixteenth notes on the recorder, before the echo kicked in, and then all eight of them would come back exactly. So I played sixteen altogether, the second set of eight in harmony with the echo's repetition of the first eight. Then the echo would do my second eight, and I'd

harmonize with *them*. If I'd known more about counterpoint I could have gone on indefinitely. The water full of dust motes, and the air full of note motes. There was inevitably some drift, and the canoe would move out of the ideal spot, so the echo would arrive late, and eventually not at all. The first couple of days, I found the spot by trial and error, paddling with one hand and tooting with the other. Then I got smart enough to fix my location with reference to points on the shore, so for the rest of the month I could find it easily. I told my family what I was doing, but it never occurred to any of us that they would come out with me and hear it. Although I was enraptured with it, obsessed by it, did little else but that in the daytime for the whole month.

Performance

A couple of weeks before Christmas, I took my violin into the nursing home and played carols for my mom. Got her into her wheelchair and took her to the auditorium, where we could make noise without disturbing anybody. I parked her in one corner, and then wandered around on the tile floor as I played, digging back in the lumberyard of my memory for the carols she liked, all the rare and beautiful ones that don't get onto the radio.

There was light coming in the window from the hall and I didn't turn on any more, so she couldn't see me crying. We both knew she was on her way out, and I felt as if I were playing her over. Across the river, through the sky, whatever it would turn out to be. I gathered tunes from our past, dragged them up from the tree-lit Christmases, eighty-seven of them for her, and floated them into the empty air of that auditorium. Forming a texture, a fabric to go with her when she got out of my reach, and had to venture bravely on by herself.

ONE EVENING, when I was four years old, a circle of the Women's Missionary Society was meeting in our living room. I was on my way to bed. My mom was doing the worship service to begin the meeting, and she was attempting to time it so that the prayer I sang every night would waft touchingly down the stairway, at just the right moment. As if from a cherub in heaven, I guess. She told me about her plan ahead of time, so I sang it as expressively as possible. *Father we thank thee for the night*, you know how it goes. An earthbound prayer, surely, in the context of my mother's worship service. Would God have listened to such a shameless piece of theatre?

Alas, I sang it too softly, so it didn't waft the distance. She came to the foot of the stairs and called up. "Are you going to sing your prayer, dear?" It was the archness in her voice, the attempt still to pass it off as an unplanned event, the inability to come clean that enraged me. "I *did* already!" I shouted down as rudely as possible. "Well would you do it again for us, dear?" I went and crouched on the carpet at the top of the stairs and spit it down, word by dratted word, in a fury. Hoping the notes would turn into missiles to maim them all.

WHAT OCCURRED in the intervening years? To bring me from that stairway carpet, crouching and angry, wanting her out of my life, to that darkened auditorium, walking barefoot on the tile and tenderly playing, crying because I knew that soon she was going to go?

After the wretched first six years of her life, my mother lived in Delaware, Ohio, with her maternal grandmother. They survived on a Civil War pension of fifteen dollars a month, and whatever the grandmother could add to that by taking in washing. My mother's other grandmother lived two blocks up the hill, where she was housekeeper for a "pufessor" who owned a big house and played the violin. He symbolized, for my mother, a way of life that was cultural, uplifting, and good.

Jump ahead thirty years, and you'll find this model providing the motive for the music lessons my brother and I took. We were having all the things she couldn't have, when she was a child. It was excessive, not surprisingly. The year I was nine I was taking piano, violin, ballet, tap dancing and drawing.

What surprises me, with that amount of pressure, is that I enjoyed music at all. There was a great deal of command performing, when company came, or when a church group meeting found itself short of entertainment. My brother sang, and played the piano. I played the piano and violin. So we could provide a variety of duet combinations. (When my brother was younger, when I was still a baby, he had played his tonette on the Saturday morning radio junior talent hour so frequently that the producers were beginning to tire of him. Sensing this, he offered one Saturday to play it with it sticking in his nose. An effect somewhat lost on radio, but they did announce it. My mother sat at home listening and died a thousand deaths.)

So it was very public. And our various audiences were completely undiscriminating. I could have a little piece, a sailor's hornpipe, say, at the peak of performing perfection, and the Women's Missionary Society would think it was wonderful. The next month I could go in with something I'd only started learning the day before and fudge my way through it, mistake-laden and with great chunks of the hard parts left out completely, and they would still think it was wonderful. Now, I don't mean to suggest that those women knew nothing about music. But the script of the little moving tableau required that when the preacher's daughter performed for you, you exclaimed at it afterwards, over tea and sandwiches, regardless of the calibre of her performance.

I'm describing this, of course, with hindsight. I understand, now, what was going on. I'm even willing to admit I was probably pretty cute. And that surely there must have been women in the audience who groaned inwardly, and thought Oh god, not this little twerp again. But at the time, can you imagine what this scenario did for my own sense of musical integrity? And do you wonder that fifteen years later I'd be happiest out alone in a canoe, playing with an echo?

But as I say, what surprises me, in that veritable soup of false adulation and guilt, where my musical progress was screamed from the rooftops for the benefit of the whole neighbourhood, is that I did enjoy it. I did manage to feel, at least part of the time, that what I was doing was private, and made a kind of sense to me inside my head, where I lived when I could get out of the spotlight.

Piano exam

I took my grade three Royal Conservatory piano exam in Vancouver. The examiner had come all the way out from Toronto. I was nervous; dressed, of course, over-fussily, and fussed over in the waiting room. The examiner was a large man, with dark glasses that obscured most of his face. He sat at a little table in the corner of the room, uttering occasional non-committal grunts like a giant toad. He told me what to play, which scales, which studies, which pieces, and I played them. He grunted. I loved one of the pieces by Handel. I don't remember what it was, it was in the Royal Conservatory book, but that's long since gone. A little ditty, anyway, a Handel tune harmonized simply enough for grade three. It wasn't related, for me, to the mechanics of playing the piano. It was more like a walk in the forest. I forgot about the toad in the corner, and just went into the woods. When I was done he took off his dark glasses and smiled at me with a pair of kind and penetrating blue eyes. I was startled to discover that he was, after all, a human being. He said, "Isn't Handel wonderful?"

I saw, in a short but vivid moment, an adult land that he must belong to, where people understood what you meant, where you could simply quietly smile and agree that you liked Handel without any flashbulbs going off. I think, looking back, that without that moment I wouldn't have survived my childhood.

The Novels of
William Maxwell

ALICE MUNRO

I FIRST READ William Maxwell in the early sixties. *They Came Like Swallows* was the first novel of his I read, and I don't think I knew how good he was. I knew he was good, but I wasn't as excited by his work then as later. After I read *So Long, See You Tomorrow* when it was published in 1980, I went back and read everything else of his over again, and I was amazed. I thought: This is how it should be done. And I thought: I wish I could go back and do everything of mine over more simply and more naturally, and with more respect. Not so that everything I wrote would sound like this, but so that it would be informed with this spirit.

William Maxwell was born in Lincoln, Illinois, in 1908. He has written five novels: *Bright Centre of Heaven*, *They Came Like Swallows*, *The Folded Leaf*, *Time Will Darken It*, *The Chateau*, and *So Long, See You Tomorrow*. And a number of stories which I've read separately, but haven't seen in a collection.

The foreword to *Time Will Darken It* is a long quotation from a sixteenth-century painter, Francisco Pacheco.

The order observed in painting a landscape . . . is as follows: First, one draws it, dividing it into three or four distances or planes. In the foremost, where one places the figure or saint, one draws the largest trees or rocks. . . . In the second, smaller trees and houses are drawn; in the third yet smaller, and in the fourth, where the mountain ridges meet the sky, one ends with the greatest diminution of all.

The drawing is followed by the blocking out or laying in of colours, which some painters are in the habit of doing in black and white, although I deem it better to execute it directly in colour. . . . If you temper the necessary quantity of pigment . . . with linseed or walnut oil and add enough white, you shall produce a bright tint. It must not be dark; on the contrary, it must be rather on the light side because time will darken it.

There are two more paragraphs of straightforward, practical instruction, but this is enough to show you Maxwell's intention. He's letting us know how he writes a novel. His method will be orderly and deliberate, painstaking and traditional. Unsurprising. Or so you think. You know where you are with this writer; the solid background—the well-developed minor characters, some nicely managed shifts in points of view. And then—it's wonderful—something new is happening. The shift is going a little further than you expect, the structure is wrenched apart. There's a new exhilaration, as if you were walking on air. And with that change in the way the novel's made, there's a sense of change in what it's about.

Time Will Darken It starts off as the story of a fairly happy, youngish, mid-Western couple, being visited by some relatives from Mississippi. It's almost a delicate domestic comedy; an evening party, a little rift in the marriage, a too-intense young girl, old maids and their mother. But by the end of the book, what has happened? The patient, honourable, somehow obtuse husband, Austin King, has been made aware that his way of managing life is hardly any good at all. The girl has fallen in love with him, and in her desperate state of mind, has had a terrible accident. For her scars and for her love, there is no cure. His wife, going into a dangerous childbirth, is not comforted or satisfied by his love, and she never will be. He feels cut off from his life. He walks through the town in the dark to the railway station.

The signal lights switched far down the tracks, south of town. The ticket agent came out of the station. His description afterward of what happened that night would in no way have paralleled or corroborated Austin King's. *Number 317 was coming a little late*, one of them would have said. The other would have said *Time was cool and flowed softly around me. I didn't like to put my head down in cold water that might not be too clean, and it was hard to swim against the current without doing that, so I drifted downstream toward the monument works and then fought my way back. Twice I tried to crawl out onto the platform but it didn't work. Each time I lost my hold. The platform, the station, the empty birdhouse, the stars, and Mike Farrell's saloon fell away from under me and I was swept downstream. The third time I put my head under water and swam straight toward the light. It was easier than I imagined. When I stopped swimming I was well within the wedge made by two parallel steel rails meeting at infinity, and the light was shining right on my face. I tried to stand up but there was no bottom. There was nothing to stand on, and when I came up for air a second I was still inside the wedge. Although I had been swimming much harder than before, I hadn't got anywhere. I was out of breath and I knew I was somewhere I had no business to be.*

You don't have to have water to drown in. All it requires is that your normal vision be narrowed down to a single point and continue long enough on that point until you begin to remember and to achieve a state of being which is identical with the broadest view of human life. You can drown in a desert, in the mountain air, in an open car at night with the undersides of the leafy branches washing over you, mile after midnight mile. All you need is a single idea, a point of intense pain, a pin-prick of light growing larger and steadier and more persuasive until the mind and the desire to live are both shattered in starry sensation, leading inevitably toward no sensation whatever. . . .

The station master said something that Austin (with the light falling all around him from a great height) did not hear. . . . *He's right, I guess. He must be right. I've known Fred Vercel for years and never knew him to say anything that wasn't so. If he did call to me, as he says—if he warned me, I probably stepped back, in plenty of time, and the rest is some kind of strange hallucination. But I never had any such feeling before. I know he spoke to me, but the way I remember it, I couldn't hear what he said. I couldn't hear anything but the sound of the approaching engine, and even that stopped when I went under. I had never been in a situation I couldn't get out of, and I held my breath and felt myself being rolled over and over, helpless, on the bottom. My mind, in an*

orderly fashion, reached one conclusion after another and I knew finally that there wasn't going to be any more for me. This was all. Here in this place. Now. And I felt the most terrible sadness because it was not the way I expected to die. It was just foolish. I shouldn't have looked into the light so long. I knew better. And I was not quite ready to die. There were certain things that I still wanted to do. I suppose everybody feels that way when their time comes.

For a second there was air over me and I opened my eyes. I was still inside the wedge. . . . This time I couldn't hold my breath. What came in or went out was beyond my control. I let go, knowing where I was, knowing that gravel touched my forehead, that I was being turned over and over, and that I would never escape from this trap alive. I came to the surface again, without struggling, and saw the two lights on the last car of the train getting smaller and smaller.

I should have waited for another train, maybe, but I didn't. I was very tired. I don't ever remember being as tired as I was that night. I'd been letting myself down. A little bit at a time, over a period of several hours I guess, I'd been letting myself down. I'd been watching what other people do, so I could learn to be more like them, and somehow—maybe because I didn't understand what I saw or it could have been that I was just too tired—it didn't seem worth the bother. I don't know how I got home. I just found myself there, looking through the dining-room window at the thermometer to see how cold it was, turning off the lights, going up the stairs to bed.

A couple of weeks later his wife comes home from the hospital with their new son. The girl has gone away, still in pain, defeated. All is well. Lying in bed beside him, the wife begins to talk about her feelings of change, her loss of faith in their marriage. But in the midst of this he goes to sleep. She gets up furious, and sits by the window holding her baby, thinking how she will leave with her children, begin a life that is poor, decent, and brave. Looking at her son she thinks how she will bring him up to be unlike his father; not to be nice, not to be polite, not to make the best of things, but in full knowledge of what life is. Finally, cold, but still wakeful and angry, she gets back into bed.

Austin stirred, and put his arm across her, and she took hold of it, by the wrist, and removed it, but when she moved away from him, towards the outer edge of the bed, he followed again in his sleep, and curled around her in a way that made her want to shout at him, and beat his face with her fists. She pushed the arm away, roughly this time, but he still did not waken. The arm had a life of its own. All the rest of him, his body and his soul, were asleep. But the arm was awake, and came across her, and the hand settled on her heart, and she let it stay there for a moment, thinking how hard and heavy it was compared to the child she had been holding, how importunate, how demanding; how it was no part of her and never would be, insisting on a satisfaction, even in sleep, that she could not give. She started to push it away once more but her own arms were bound to the bed. Only her mind was awake, able to act, to hate. And then suddenly the delicate gold chain of awareness, no stronger than its weakest link, gave way. Circled by the body next to her, enclosed in warmth, held by the arm that knew (even though the man it belonged to did not), Martha King was asleep.

I HAVEN'T TIME to talk about *They Came Like Swallows*, which is about the death of a young mother, or *The Folded Leaf*, which is a marvellous novel about two adolescent boys turning into men, and the friendship between them turning into something they cannot bear. I'll just talk about *So Long, See You Tomorrow*, which is also about the friendship of two boys, and the betrayal of friendship, and about the death of a mother, and the subsequent disintegration of the family.

The inappropriate, helpless, destructive sexual passion is there too, and the outcome here is darker than in the earlier novels with their near suicides and humbled reconciliations. Here, the suicide is preceded by a murder, and there isn't even the hope that it can fail. But this classic, predictable drama of passion is framed in the story of the two boys, their unexpected friendship, their survival. It is also seen at one stage (and I don't know any other writer who would try this, let alone get away with it) through the eyes of a dog. Events have got to the point where the family has broken up. They can't take the dog with them; she's left on the farm for the new tenant.

The borrowed model T drove off down the lane, and the dog was tied up, with night coming on, and no lights in the house, and no smoke going up the chimney.

She waited a long long time, trying not to worry. Trying to be good—trying to be especially good. And telling herself that they had only gone in to town and were coming right back, even though it was perfectly obvious that this wasn't true. Not the way they acted. Eventually, in spite of her, the howls broke out. Sit-ting on her haunches, with her muzzle raised to the night sky, she howled and howled. And it wasn't just the dog howling, it was all the dogs she was descended from, clear back to some wolf or other.

She heard footsteps and was sure it was the boy: *He had heard her howling and had come from wherever it was he had been all* this time *and was going to rescue her. . . .*

It turned out to be the man's friend from over the way. He put his lantern on the ground and untied her and talked to her and stroked her ears, and for a minute or two everything was all right. But then she remembered how they didn't tell her to get in the car with them but drove off without even a backward look, and she let out another despairing howl.

Lloyd Wilson tried to get her to go home with him but she couldn't. If she did that, who would be on hand there to guard the property?

In a little while he was back with some scraps for her, which she swallowed so fast that she didn't know afterward what it was she'd eaten. He filled the bowl with water from the pump and left it by the door of her house. Then he called to her and whistled, but she wouldn't budge. "Have it your own way, but I doubt if anybody's going to get a wink of sleep," he said cheerfully, and went off into the darkness.

She howled at intervals all night, and set the other dogs in the neighbourhood to barking. The next day when the man's friend came to see how she was getting on, she went halfway to meet him, wagging her behind. . . .

That night at supper, with the dog sitting beside the chair and listening as if the story was about her, Lloyd Wilson said, "You never had to tell him anything. When he died, I swore I'd never have another. . . ."

The dog raised her head suddenly. Then she got up and went to the door: a wagon or cart had turned into the lane at her place. She whined softly, but nobody paid any attention until there were footsteps outside and she started barking. "Be quiet, Trixie," Lloyd Wilson said and pushed his chair back from the table. In the light from the open door he saw a young man who looked as if he were about ready to start running.

"Name's Walker," he said. "I'm your new neighbour. . . . You haven't seen anything of my dog, have you?"

Seeing the rope dangling from the tree, James Walker kept the dog tied up for the next two days, though he had been assured it wasn't necessary. But he also fed her and saw that her pan had water in it and talked to her sometimes. And when night came there was a light in the kitchen window, and the dog smelled wood smoke. Things could have been worse. From time to time she wanted to howl, and managed not to. The day after that, trucks came, bringing cattle and hogs and farm machinery and furniture. And that evening the young man untied the rope and said, "Come on, old girl, I need you to help me around the cows." She understood what he said all right, but she wasn't his old girl, and she lit off down the road as fast as lightning.

In this same novel we find the narrator, one of those boys grown old, looking at a sculpture in the museum of modern art. It is "Palace at 4 a.m.," by Giacometti. A spare, strange structure of thin uprights and horizontal beams, in which there is something like a flying bird, the backbone of an animal, a female figure, and a hollowed-out spatulate shape with a ball in front of it. The narrator is reminded of the new house that his father and stepmother were building when the events of the story took place. He quotes again from the artist's own notes on his work.

"This object took shape little by little in the late summer of 1932; it revealed itself to me slowly, the various parts taking their exact form and their precise place within the hole. By autumn it had attained such reality that its actual execution in space took no more than one day. It is related without any doubt to a period in my life that had come to an end a year before, when for six whole months hour after hour was passed in the company of a woman who, concentrating all life in herself, magically transformed my every moment. We used to construct a fantastic palace at night—days and nights had the same colour, as if everything happened just before daybreak; throughout the whole time I never saw the sun—a very fragile palace of matchsticks. At the slightest false move a whole section of this tiny construction would collapse. We would always begin it over again. I don't know why it came to be inhabited by a spinal column in a cage—the spinal column this woman sold me one of the very first nights I met her on the street—and by one of the skeleton birds that flutter with cries of joy at four o'clock in the morning very high above the pool of clear, green water where the extremely fine, white skeletons of fish float in the great unroofed hall. In the middle there rises the scaffolding of a tower, perhaps unfinished or, since its top has collapsed, perhaps also broken. On the other side there appeared the statue of a woman, in which I recognise my mother, just as she appears in my earliest memories. The mystery of her long black dress touching the floor troubled me; it seemed to me like a part of her body, and aroused in me a feeling of fear and confusion. . . ."

Now the narrator continues:

I seem to remember that I went to the new house one winter day and saw snow descending through the attic to the upstairs bedrooms. It could also be that I never did any such thing, for I am fairly certain that in a snapshot album I have lost track of there was a picture of the house taken in the circumstances I have just described, and it is possible that I am remembering that rather than an actual experience. What we, or at any rate what I, refer to confidently as memory—meaning a moment, a scene, a fact that has been subjected to a fixative and thereby rescued from oblivion—is really a form of storytelling that goes on continually in the mind and often changes with the telling. Too many conflicting emotional interests are involved for life ever to be wholly acceptable, and possibly it is the work of the storyteller to rearrange things so that they conform to this end. In any case, in talking about the past we lie with every breath we draw.

THERE YOU ARE. The simple, banal, terrible story and its mysterious heart.

William Maxwell died this past summer. Alice Munro's essay originally appeared in Brick *in 1988.*

The Mind's Eye:
Thoughts on Filmmaking and Writing

TISSA ABEYSEKARA

I AM A FILMMAKER who has written a novel. That novel, *Bringing Tony Home* was my first foray into English writing, four years ago, and has yet to be followed up with anything substantial—at least in print. I am still very much a filmmaker, one whose entire youth has been spent in the service of the moving image, learning and trying to communicate in pictures—I am tempted to say "images," but that has a wider meaning; even poetry has images; pictures, or to be more precise moving pictures, is more film specific, and one of the issues I am going to talk about, is the difference between the image in film and the image in literature. Many people tell me that my book, *Bringing Tony Home* is very visual. They imply and sometimes state quite specifically, this may be due to my upbringing in films. I am not so sure. I do not wish to quote from my book, but here's a passage from a novel, a finely crafted story, not by someone who is known as a writer—though he is supposed to write beautifully in his native language—but as one of the greatest moviemakers of all time:

It is the last Sunday in July, 1925, a hot sunny afternoon in Stockholm. The church in the tower above the cupola strikes half past three. The streets are deserted. A tram is making its way laboriously up the hill along the West Side of the churchyard bordering on the spacious square with its indoor market and theatre. At the top, a woman gets off and stands there.

Anna.

She is wearing a beige suit, the ankle-length skirt a slightly darker colour, high-heeled boots and a simple shady hat. Her jacket is open over a high-necked lace blouse. She is wearing no jewellery, except her wedding ring and small diamond ear-rings. She is clutching her pale leather handbag to her, her thin gloves carelessly thrust into the jacket pockets.

She takes off her hat and holds it in her left hand. Her thick dark hair is parted in the middle and gathered into a low knot that has begun to loosen. Her eyes are dark brown below the strongly drawn eyebrows and low broad forehead. Her mouth is large, the lips friendly and generous.

These are the opening lines of the great Swedish moviemaker Ingmar Bergman's remarkable first novel, *Private Confessions*, and isn't it very visual? But there is something beyond the physical reality described with such photographic accuracy; there is a subtext; it is not a report of what the naked eye sees, but a reflection of the mind's eye which makes the passage so evocative inspite of the spare undecorative prose. However, all the shades and the tones are encoded in the words themselves; in the way they are composed together. Because language by its very nature is thick with associations. It bears on itself the collective thoughts, feelings, and emotions of the billions of minds and hearts of those who have spoken it through hundreds or even thousands of years. A moving picture can acquire such richness of texture and meaning only through a conscious synthesis with other elements. When a filmmaker places his camera defining the spatial relationship between the recording instrument and the object it records, creating a certain perspective; when he deliberately moulds the light to invest the object or the frame with a certain ambience; when an image thus manipulated and recorded is juxtaposed with another such image, and he adds sound by way of music or carefully orchestrated natural effects, he does nothing more than attempt to invest his picture with the same associative power of language; to artificially manufacture a subtext. In other words he is trying to recreate not what his physical eye has seen but what his mind's eye has observed, felt and reflected. For the poet, his raw material comes to him processed, fine-tuned, prepared, and preordained. For the filmmaker, there is a painful and laborious process of moulding the clay before he begins to create and to communicate.

This has created a problem, which is central to most film criticism, even at its best. Most often the preparatory process is treated as the creative act, mainly because both occur in full view of the spectator. The very nature of the medium makes it near impossible to hide the mechanism, the invisibility of which is one of the prerequisites of good art. Or, is this transparency, the display of the manipulation, the cunning, something desirable in a Brechtian sense? The issue is open for debate. The aesthetics of film is divided between the theory of montage as spelt out by the great guru, the Russian Eisenstein and the marvellously incisive musings on the cinema by André Bazin, the Frenchman who spoke of the image as being evaluated not according to what it adds to reality but what it reveals of it. Eisenstein argued that the plastics of the image and its juxtaposition with another should invest the image with a meaning not intrinsic to it.

In the last five decades cinema seems to have drifted more towards the gospel according to Bazin, and what is so heartening to those who seek to invest the moving image with the same evocative power as the word is that in the works of filmmakers like Yasujiro Ozu of Japan, Robert Bresson of France and André Tarkovsky of Russia there is a perfect fusion between manipulation and the creative act. The image is purified almost to the point of minimalism but exudes a tremendous evocative power. The visual language of these films acquire the kind of translucent simplicity, best described by Regi Siriwardena in his wonderful monograph on poetry "In The Pure Water Of Poetry." Regi refers to a lecture on Wordsworth's poetry by the late Professor E F C Ludowyke, wherein he quotes from a little known critic by the name of Ian Jack to define the essential quality of the English poet who had till then occupied a lower shelf to Milton, Keats, and Shelley; "the glass seems empty because it is so full of pure water."

THIS IS A GOOD POINT at which to come back to language.

The act of creative writing is not an easy one. But once you discover you can write, it becomes easier than making a movie. Here I don't mean only the physical exercise, where the difference between writing and moviemaking is enormous. "Filmmaking," according to David Lean, "is the toughest job after coal mining." Writing is such a private affair, a communion with life both holy and personal. That demands stamina of a different sort. But I wish to draw your attention to another aspect, something often overlooked and never fully understood. This is the relative ease with which a writer—provided he has a reasonable command of the language in which he is writing and of course imagination—could create a mood or obtain an effect, than a filmmaker who may have a good command of his craft and also the gift. The reason for this I have already hinted at; it is quite simply the power and richness of language as an instrument of evocation and a conveyor of feeling, thought and emotion.

Some may disagree of course. A single picture is better than a thousand words, goes the well known adage. I will not disagree. But there is a deeper issue here. The issue is the subtle and sometimes not-so-subtle difference between our need to be convinced of the authenticity of what we see as a reproduction, and the need to be moved, emotionally. This is the difference between the indexical realism of Emile Zola and the psychological truth of a Dostoevsky. There is a simple rule to be observed when writing a film script which illustrates the point I am trying to make. In a screenplay, thou shall not write anything that cannot be seen nor heard. Now that excludes a good part of modern and post-modern fiction from Joyce and Woolf to Gabriel Garcia Marquez, Italo Calvino, and Rushdie. It also raises a severe suspicion: if by the aforementioned rule of film scriptwriting it is an exercise restricted to the portrayal of superficial reality—that which can be seen or heard—can film be taken seriously?

There are innumerable instances to be quoted as examples where moviemakers have transcended this severe limitation and brought film to the level of high art. Nevertheless this was achieved not through the exploitation of any properties intrinsic to the image itself, but through the deft manipulation of elements extraneous to it—in most instances through the clever use of sound.

Literature, though, in the view of Eisenstein, is, 'that land where, although not perhaps its birthplace, the cinema certainly found the soil in which to grow to unprecedented and unimagined dimensions'

In a brilliant and oft-quoted essay, titled "Dickens, Griffith & the Film Today," Eisenstein argues quite convincingly that there was no immaculate conception where the birth of the cinema was concerned; it was quite simply born out of the womb of nineteenth century realistic fiction. In the great big sprawling and lusty novels of Charles Dickens, which combine the romantic and the picaresque of the age of Cervantes with the harsh grey realism of industrial England, Eisenstein observes the basic symptoms of a future form of expression. He quotes the whole of Chapter XXI of *Oliver Twist*, the long way along the Bethnal Green Road, as the day breaks slowly through the fog; the street lamps winking in the grey light of dawn; the crowds accumulating on the way; the noise, the crowd, increasing gradually as the market comes nearer.

This, to Eisenstein, was montage at its cinematic best, and it preshadows the visual language of David Wark Griffith, who in America in the first two decades of the twentieth century, was pushing the primitive magic of the nickelodeon into the realm of an epic art form.

Thus film, in the gospel according to Eisenstein, may have its roots in literature; to be more specific, in the Victorian novel which is strong in visual quality. But the novel has moved beyond the Dickensian form, and in the works of the great modernists of the first half the twentieth century—William Faulkner, André Gide, Marcel Proust, James Joyce, Franz Kafka, and Virginia Woolf, we are deep into the landscape of the mind, which no camera has the capacity to reach. It's a realm of the senses accessible only to language. Faulkner is a tremendously visual writer in that great American epic vein, but he is not photographic; what is described with such over-powering poetic intensity eludes the most sophisticated lens and when the great poets of the cinema like Kurosawa, Bergman, and Tarkovsky achieve such levels of artistic sophistication, I am sure they were the results of hard labour, and collective effort.

Now I come back to the point I made at the beginning: writing, if you have the gift for it, is easier than making movies; an artist who has trained himself, or has the gift to use language as his medium of expression has an advantage over the filmmaker. This does not make movies a lesser art form, but a more difficult one.

THIS LONG PREFACE was to pave the way for a confession. After serving the cinema almost exclusively for well over three decades, I have suddenly found writing much easier than making a movie. This may seem obvious to those who are familiar with the technical, financial, and physical demands of moviemaking. But the problem lay beyond such practical matters. It is in the nature of the creative act itself and the respective abilities of the picture and the word to probe and reach beyond mere superficial reality. This is what I have in my own way tried to explain so far. Film is still very near and dear to me. After all these years and with many rich and beautiful memories associated with the movies, film is in my bloodstream. Nevertheless I am beginning to find immense pleasure in writing, as much pleasure as I get when making a film. Both are jealous mistresses, and right now I am not sure which one deserves greater attention.

But I have another and more serious problem, a problem which is endemic to me, or so I think. If I have suddenly found it easier and sometimes more pleasant to work in the written word, I have also discovered that I am more at ease not in my mother tongue of Sinhala, but in English. This bothers me.

I do not wish to delve into the peculiar circumstances of my life which has made me bi-lingual—or as I would like to say "double-tongued". But there are some thoughts which have nagged me in the last few years. These thoughts relate to the situation where someone whose mother tongue is Sinhala, and in which language he has grown up for well over forty years, finds himself articulating his innermost feelings and recapturing the most intimate of memories in English with reasonable sincerity and conviction. When I won the Gratiaen Prize for *Bringing Tony Home*, a publisher offered me a substantial amount of money for a Sinhala translation. I accepted the offer but fortunately and perhaps wisely did not accept the mandatory advance. I had presumed it would be the easiest of things. I was proved wrong. The first three pages were a struggle, and then to my dismay I found the translation flat and laboured. The story was getting bleached of its subtext and the writing was becoming quite false and mechanical, Now this was a strange situation. How could an experience so steeped in Sri Lankan life, though written originally in English, lose its flavour when translated into the language which is intrinsic to the story and its socio-cultural backdrop? I gave up translating. But the issue kept nagging me. I kept asking myself why I wrote the story in English, in the first place, and why when writing it I found it so easy to recapture the memories in a language that was not my mother tongue.

Of course the experience recounted in *Bringing Tony Home* is from that early phase of my life when

English was very much part of my daily life. But then there was that traumatic break when overnight I was plucked away and thrust into a milieu where English was never spoken. I do not wish to credit myself with an abnormal facility to store away in some corner of my memory the subtle tones, nuances, shades of meaning of a language which had ceased to be a part of my life for very nearly twenty years. That would be akin to Anna Akhmatova's historic feat of storing in her memory for forty years all the poems she composed during the Stalinist re-

pression. No, I had to seek an answer elsewhere. I have reached a conclusion which may be considered blasphemous traitorous, and even vile by my Sinhala colleagues. But I wish to declare it frankly, sincerely, and bluntly. To hell with the consequences.

The Sinhala language has stopped growing. It is frozen somewhere in the late fifties, and in the service of power politics, dishonest and cheap journalism, and merchandising, has been degenerating ever since. Reaching supreme heights of poetic expression and philological muscle in the great literary renaissance of sixteenth century Kotte, the Sinhala language lived its last great moment of evolution in Martin Wickramasingha, Munidasa Kumaratunga, and Sarachchandra. The crisis in the Sinhala language is best reflected in the realm of fiction where nothing of great substance has been written in the last four decades.

Fiction, in contemporary Sinhala literature, emerged as a serious art form with Martin Wickramasingha's *Gamperaliya* in 1943 and reached its peak with *Viragaya* by the same author, in 1956. In between, the Sinhala novel enlisted in its ranks some fine exponents like Sarachchandra, Gunadasa Amarasekara, and G.B. Senanayake. But none of them even at their best could surpass the pioneer, Wickramasingha. Trapped in the aesthetic of the realistic novel, especially of the nineteenth century Russian model and the critical values of post-revolutionary Soviet social realism, those of the second generation after Wickramasingha began a process of decline which continues even today. In the contemporary Sinhala novel, the level of social and psychological observation is superficial, the craft both in narrative construction and dramatic structure is hackneyed and at times downright amateurish, the quality of writing is journalistic. The victim is language. Or is it the other way around? The language seems anaemic and inadequate to convey experience which is meaningful both in terms of life and art.

IT WAS MARTIN WICKRAMASINGHA who almost singlehandedly forged an idiom out of the heavily sanskritised tendentious and florid linguistic style of the early twentieth century Sinhala writers. His style, a wonderful mixture of the written and the spoken idiom, closed the gap between the rhetoric of classical Sinhala, which had lost its popular base, and the simple cadences, rhythms and tones of rural speech. I must emphasize the word "rural" here because the style of Martin Wickramasingha is rooted in and carved out of the texture of life of his beloved Koggala, which till WW II was part of Sri Lankan arcadia. Wickramasingha's prose was at its expressive best when the themes, the situations, and the drama were set in the village. In *Viragaya*, which is located both in time and space in a twilight world between the village and the rapidly spreading urbania, Wickramasingha's poetic sensibility has reached its borderline. He did not pro-

ceed beyond. Gunadasa Amarasekara was the last major talent to work within the aesthetic as prepared by his great predecessor, but then the great big themes waiting for the Sinhala novelist had shifted to the city. The language of Sinhala fiction which had blossomed in the sweet arbours and valleys, "far from the madding crowd" could not reflect the harsh, grainy, and fragmented reality of Sri Lankan urbania. There was no Eliot, no Hemingway. Sinhala creative fiction began a process of inbreeding, of subsisting on its own body like the mythical serpent in Sanskrit legend. Into the vacuum came a generation of writers who had no great models to fall back upon, and because of linguistic constraints, no points of inspiration to draw from, creative fiction became bland reportage; puerile polemics became the order of the day. In the process the Sinhala language has degenerated to the point where it no longer seems to have the ring of truth. There is a gap between the semantics and the idea it tries to convey. The language has been devalued. The great Prachina tradition of classical linguistic knowledge is out of step with the times. Modern writing is laboured, artificial, and counterfeit.

When language becomes debased it ceases to be the conveyor of truth and loses credibility. Political rhetoric and propaganda, commercialism and religious fundamentalism have bleached the Sinhala language of its rich associative power. This has happened in the last three decades, because the language has not been able to adapt itself to the vast socio-cultural transition that has taken place. What has happened is the frightening debasement of the existing currency of words through misuse. There is an example I never tire of quoting. In the Sinhala language there is a word for "incomparable" which has a very sacred connotation, for it is used only when referring to the Buddha. There was a TV commercial which used this word when referring to the quality of a toothbrush. When the same vocabulary is used to sell consumer products and preach moral values something happens to the semantics.

I am not a religious fanatic, but as one who deals with words in my profession, I am respectful of the associative shades of meaning, for otherwise I fail in my communication. The biggest debasers and corrupters of the language have been the politicians. I can speak only about the Sinhala language with any kind of authority. Over half a century of political dishonesty has entered the bloodstream of the Sinhala language like a virus. I think the rot began in the immediate postwar years, when Sri Lankan society woke up from years of seclusion, imposed by the Colonial rulers, to realise that the world has changed forever. Forced with the crucial task of "catching up" with the lost years, Sri Lankan society has been taking a series of wrong turns. The transitory phase of Dominion Status, a kind of probationary period before the Commonwealth was born, gave way to total independence in 1948. Just at this point there was a fatal split between the National Movement which drew inspiration from a Sinhala Buddhist base which had emerged as an organised force in the last years of the nineteenth century, and the Left Movement led by a brilliant galaxy of young intellectuals, tutored by Western academia, and with strong middle-class roots. Politics and culture sprang apart. Social revolution and national liberation took different paths. The left movement in Sri Lanka was predominantly Trotskyite, and that brand of Marxism, it has to be accepted, was the most hostile to Nationalism. The concepts of Class Struggle, Permanent Revolution, and Capital Accumulation, being totally alien, were translated into hollow and meaningless shibboleths. Thus was created a communication gap between those who aspired to rule and the vast mass of the people. It was closed in the immediate post war years, by the right wing politicians, inheritors of the Buddhist revivalism of the late nineteenth and early twentieth century, in whose hands culture, in the exclusively Buddhist-Sinhala sense, became heavily politicised. Language suffered the most.

The Sinhala language became not only an instrument of political intrigue it was also an icon of religious fundamentalism, and cultural chauvinism. Ancient and hallowed usages, idioms heavy with human values, legends and myths which reflected love and compassion in the genuine Buddhist spirit were diluted with narrow sectarianism, and racial animosity. On the one hand the Sinhala language was withdrawing into a shell of "Aryanism," and on the other its voice was losing clarity and honesty in a babel of foreign roots and borrowings.

The cancer has continued unabated. With the passing away of the great talents—referred to earlier—the Sinhala language has become a murky backwater covered with the algae of cheap political expression and third rate tendenzpoesie. It constantly frustrates genuine poetic expression, and the honest portrayal of life.

The problem has been compounded by another irrevocable factor.

The Sinhala language had developed its grammer and its syntax, its semantics and its tone in close association with Buddhism. It has a subtext which is essentially Buddhistic in feeling. How could such a language become the common vehicle for a community which lost its religious homogeneity in the sixteenth century? And its agro-centric character to the sweeping urbanity that developed much acceleration in the eighties?

The national revival in the nineteenth and early twentieth centuries was a reactivation of these fundamental qualities in our language and culture. There was no corresponding and intelligent attempt to come to terms with the emerging world order. As we celebrate the fiftieth anniversary of our independence from colonial rule we are yet to find a solution to our central dilemma: to transform the Sinhala language from its essentially Buddhistic and agro-centric texture and heart to become the voice of a modern pluralistic society.

In the songs of Ananda Samarakoon and Sunil Shantha—inspired by the Tagorean example; the theatre of Sarachchandra—lovingly wrought from the elements of folk drama; the Dance of Chitrasena, and the best of Lester James Peries in cinema, there is a harmony of the elements, because they deal essentially with arcadia, with a rural life style where culture still retains the unity between language and life. But that landscape is no more. Martin Wickramasinghe's beloved Koggala—as central to all his novels as Malgudi is to the writings of R. K. Narayan—hums and reverberates to the sound of a thousand machines in a Free Trade Zone; Chitrasena's waterfront in his pathbreaking ballet. "Karadiya" rattles with the sound of a thousand outboard motors; Sunil Shantha's "Lily Pond" in a song that is at the heart of every Sri Lankan, lay under a hundred highrises.

ALL THESE REFLECTIONS passed through my mind as I attempted to translate my little book into the language in which it should really have been written in the first instance.

How could an alien tongue which still bears within it associations of colonialism and class discrimination be the surrogate, one may ask. It is my feeling that the English language comes to us free of all its Anglo-Saxon associations. It comes to us neutral and we, depending on the way we use it, could invest it with fresh meaning and association. I quote Salman Rushdie from his essay "Imaginary Homelands":

Many have referred to the argument about the appropriateness of English to Indian themes. And I hope all of us share the view that we simply cannot use the language in the way the

British did; that it needs remaking for our own purposes. Those of us who do use English in spite of our ambiguity towards it, or perhaps because of that, do so perhaps because we can find in that linguistic struggle a reflection of other struggles taking place in the real world, struggles between the cultures within ourselves and the influences at work upon our societies. To conquer English may be to complete the process of making ourselves free.

Contained in that paragraph is all that I have laboured to express in the second part of this essay. But I think there is an underlying thread which runs through from the beginning, however tenuously. In my shift from the moving image to the written—or perhaps even the spoken—word, and in the accompanying act of adopting English, as my primary mode and language of expression, there is perhaps an attempt to come to terms, reconcile and transcend the social, cultural, and class conflicts which are my legacy. There is a need to hack through myths and growths and seek the rosebud of truth. This is not an idealistic pursuit, nor even an intellectual search. It is pure and simple, an act of survival.

Our tragedy today is a general and universal physical fear so long sustained by now that we can even bear it. There are no longer problems of the spirit. There is only the question: When will I be blown up? Because of this, the young man or woman writing today has forgotten the problem of the human heart in conflict with itself which alone can make good writing because only that is worth writing about, worth the agony and the sweat.

I wish I could have written that. But that's a quote. It was spoken half a century ago on the tenth of December 1950 in Stockholm, by one of the greatest novelists of the twentieth century, William Faulkner in his Speech of Acceptance upon the award of the Nobel Prize for Literature.

How valid those sentiments are for today, and for us in hither Sri Lanka!

I may sound like one who is speaking at the end of his career. I have only just begun, though rather late in life when I have much less time left than what I have lived so far. But in the few years ahead of me I wish to dedicate myself to serving those values so beautifully and simply expressed by William Faulkner.

Heian Holiday

MICHAEL DIRDA

Washington's cherry blossoms have already faded, and once again I failed to see them during the short period of their fleeting beauty. Perhaps it's just as well. I would have wandered among the branches heavy with flowers and thought somber thoughts about the passage of the years and the transitoriness of life, surrendering to that sweet sorrow which the Japanese call *mono no aware*:

> As he wandered from one familiar spot to another it affected him strangely to find those whom he had recently thought of as mere children playing the part of dignified masters and possessors amid the scenes where he himself had once submitted to his elders' rule.

> For days it had rained unceasingly. But now, just at the moment when the heavy rain stopped and only a few scattered drops were falling, the moon rose; and soon it was one of those exquisite late spring nights through whose stillness he had in earlier years so often ridden out on errands of adventure.

> Again and again Murasaki told herself that life was very short. Soon this and all else would be over; what sense could there be in minding things so much?

> A mist lay over the hills and outlined against it was the figure of a heron stiffly poised on a bare ledge of rock. The bridge lay shimmering in the mist, looking a long way off. Now and again a boat would pass under it, laden with timber. A strange, a haunting place—this Uji.

A STRANGE, a haunting book this *Genji Monogatari*—*The Tale of Genji*—from which all these quotations come. Written during the Heian renaissance of the early eleventh century, Murasaki Shikubu's classic—twice the length of *War and Peace*—has often been called the first psychological novel; it is certainly the supreme Japanese work of art, the model and inspiration for much later drama, poetry, and fiction, the subject, it is said, of more than ten thousand book-length works of criticism. For some time a scholarly friend, John Auchard, had been urging me to read this masterpiece, and over the years I had gradually acquired, in various used bookshops, the six volumes of Arthur Waley's famous translation (1926-33). Somewhere I'd also picked up a hefty trade paperback of Edward Seidensticker's more accurate and scholarly English version (1973), as well as a hardback copy of Ivan Morris's magnificent background study, *The World of the Shining Prince* (1964). These were central texts. To further prepare myself, I eagerly read Donald Keene's incisive paperback *Japanese Literature*, studied the chapter on Genji in Keene's monumental history of early Japanese literature, *Seeds in the Heart*, and paid hard cash for a copy of *The Princeton Companion to Classical Japanese Literature*. I was ready for a great reading adventure—if only I could find the time. Quite a lot of time.

Was it Napoleon or Ben Franklin who said, "I will prepare myself and my chance will come"? Years passed, and I was beginning to think that I might end up like one of the minor characters in *Genji*: "But while he was still impatiently counting the months and days that must elapse before his schemes could be fulfilled, death suddenly carried him off, and the dream of his life, which was that one at least of his daughters should be accepted at the Palace, had now no prospect of being fulfilled." But I was to be luckier than Higekuro. In January 1996 the *Washington Post* awarded me a four-week fellowship to study at Duke University, and, blithely abandoning work, family, adult responsibilities, and

the Washington winter, I took a slow train down to Durham and soon lost myself in Heian Japan.

As the Buddhist priest Kenko wrote in his *Essays in Idleness*, "the pleasantest of all diversions is to sit alone under the lamp, a book spread out before you, and to make friends with people of a distant past you have never known." Most days at Duke I would get up around 8 a.m., shower, dress, and browse around in Keene's history while munching my cornflakes and sipping coffee. Then I would trudge across the West campus to the Sanford Center, where I passed most of the daylight hours working on My Secret Writing Project, with interruptions for lunch, occasional classes, and an hour at the gym. Come 6 P.M. I would meander back to my little apartment, prepare a bachelor supper (bagel and scrambled eggs or store-bought barbecued chicken or a big salad), followed by a glass of wine and a little channel surfing. (Rather to my surprise, I discovered that there is virtually nothing worth watching on television even if you do get cable.) Then from 8 o'clock until 11 or so, I would read *Genji*, usually pausing midway to have a cup of instant coffee. Around midnight I would crawl into bed, insert a cassette into a tape player (borrowed from my number one son), and drift off to sleep to the strains of *H.M.S. Pinafore* or Dvorák's "American" quartet. The next day I would get up at 8 and do it all over again.

IT WAS OBVIOUSLY WONDERFUL, though after the first week just slightly pervaded with the melancholy of the temporary and evanescent: In nine more days, eight more days, seven more days, I must return to the real world. Still, for nearly a month I deeply enjoyed myself—in my fashion. I used *Genji* as my intellectual base, but before long I was branching out, reading J. Thomas Rimer's *Guide to Japanese Literature* and Earl Miner's *The Japanese Tradition in British and American Literature*, William Puette's (rather unsatisfying) *Reader's Guide to* The Tale of Genji and Richard Bowring's fine Cambridge Landmarks of World Literature monograph on Murasaki. I checked out a score of books from the Duke library (including a delightful collection of memoirs and appreciations of Arthur Waley), skimmed studies of Japanese diaries and Japanese court poetry, consulted the notes in scholarly tomes, photocopied essays from journals. I even listened to early koto music. Soon I also began to dip into the witty Sei Shonagon, whose *Pillow Book* revealed a soulmate's liking for lists ("Unsuitable Things," "Poetic Subjects," "Things That Should Be Short"), and who was, in some ways, Murasaki's rival (the two served competing empresses). On one memorable night, while page-surfing though Keene's *Anthology of Japanese Literature*, I fell hard for the amorous Ono no Komachi, one of whose poems I memorized in Japanese:

The flowers withered,
Their color faded away,
While meaninglessly
I spent my days in the world
And the long rains were falling.

Most of all I became entranced by the aesthetic sensibility embodied in so many Japanese words, and I was soon copying out definitions into a notebook. *Yugen*—"a kind of ethereal and profound beauty, one that lurks beneath the surface of things, unamenable to direct expression." *Eiga*—"the love of colour and grandeur, of pomp and circumstance." *Mujokan*—the Buddhist sense of the transitoriness of worldly things. *Miyabi*—courtly beauty, elegance. *Sabi*—"the desolation and beauty of loneliness; solitude, quiet." *Aware*—a sensitivity to "the tears in things." *Utsutsu*—reality; *Yume*—dream. *Yume no Ukihashi*—The Floating Bridge of Dreams. This last serves as the title for the final chapter of *Genji*; it is, of course, life itself that is the bridge of dreams.

What I came to enjoy most deeply about *The Tale of Genji* is the very fact that nothing much really happens in it. As Murasaki herself writes, "it was indeed a moment in the history of our country when the whole energy of the nation seemed to be concentrated upon the search for the prettiest method of mounting paper-scrolls."

The novel's action is almost entirely given over to Genji's disruptive love affairs, filled out with court intrigues (mostly involving marriage), beautiful descriptions of landscape and weather, Proustian depictions of jealousy, elaborate set pieces detailing religious dances and rituals, and accounts of artistic competitions. The book is unfailingly interesting without being in the least exciting or suspenseful: One watches Prince Genji—the Shining One—as time after time he discovers a beautiful young woman in some out-of-the-way spot, falls for her, and then slowly resolves the various complications that this entanglement leads to.

On occasion, Genji discovers that he has overstepped the bounds: His very brief affair with the Empress Fujitsubo (his stepmother) serves as the template for several other characters' later, equally forbidden passions. There are two or three Gothic moments—for instance, when the evil spirit of Lady Rokujo destroys the fragile beauty Yugao—and even bits of comedy, such as the portrait of a countrified nobleman who pushes his daughter at the prince and a scene in which monks mistake a beautiful young girl for a spectral were-fox.

Perhaps the single most dramatic, and utterly unexpected, sentence in the whole book occurs at the very beginning of Volume V: "Genji was dead, and there was no one to take his place." The final third of the novel chronicles the rivalry in love between the self-centered, neurotic Kaoru (thought to be Genji's son) and the self-confident womanizer Niou (Genji's grandson). In these chapters, both darker and more artfully organized than the Genji sections, Murasaki relates a series of almost Hardy-like love tragedies, all set against the ominous background of the swirling waters of the river at Uji.

"How swiftly the locks rust, the hinges grow stiff on doors that close behind us!" The month at Duke flew by, but I still vividly remember the morning when it was raining so hard that I decided to stay home in my apartment and read all day. The thunderstorm raged outside, but I sat snug in my chair, hour after happy hour. I remember thinking how strange it was that already in the eleventh century, in the middle of the world's first novel, Genji was saying that his adventures sounded "like something out of an old romance." I remember thinking too that modern feminist critics should be studying Heian literature, since virtually all its greatest authors were women.

Most of all, reading Waley's beautiful translation, I marvelled at the sentences: "'Were you now to die, I think I should soon follow you . . .' He paused, but there was no reply; for she had died suddenly like a candle blown out by the wind, and he was left in bewilderment and misery." I enjoyed Murasaki's occasional addresses to the reader—a human voice speaking directly across a thousand years: "I would indeed have been glad to carry my story a little further, but at this moment my head is aching and I am feeling very tired and depressed."

Above all, I admired the subtle ways Murasaki evokes the destructive power of eros, without ever being sexually explicit: "She was only a singularly handsome girl, looking up at him with a shy, questioning yet almost trustful air. His good resolutions suddenly broke down. Soon the world and its inhabitants seemed nothing to him, nor would he have stretched out a hand to save them from instant destruction."

Discovering *The Tale of Genji* has been one of the great literary revelations of my life. If I could, I'd like nothing better than to start rereading it immediately, this time in Seidensticker's translation.

But I doubt that I will ever again be able to re-create the nearly ideal conditions of my mini-sabbatical at Duke. For four weeks I lost myself in a book in a way that normal adult life rarely allows. And such a book, so filled with *eiga* and *yugen* and *aware*! Even now, two months later, I feel deeply grateful simply to have had the chance to experience such a great masterpiece. "At last the moon rose and it was time for the music to begin."

MARGARET ATWOOD

Things That Must Not Be Forgotten

an excerpt

MICHAEL DAVID KWAN

I CONTRACTED TRACHOMA AGAIN, more severely than the time before. The illness made for a long, painful, lonely summer circumscribed by the stone wall around our hill-top. When the bandages finally were removed, and the searing pain of sunlight bored into my brain, I sought out the shaded calm of the tree house.

To my surprise, the house next door, which had been boarded up for years, was being cleaned and painted inside and out. Gardeners were mowing the overgrown lawns and turning flower beds; bricklayers and carpenters were constructing a gazebo close to the wall that separated our houses.

"An admiral, the new commander of the naval base, has taken the house," Father said matter-of-factly at dinner. He knew this long before the workmen appeared, of course, but shielded Mother from the disturbing news as long as possible. The question on her mind—on all our minds—centred on the radio transmitter hidden in our coal shed, and the nocturnal rendezvous held at our house with other members of the resistance.

Father was not perturbed. "The admiral's proximity is actually an advantage," he reasoned. "Who would dream clandestine activities were happening under his nose! Of course, precautions have to be taken. The important thing is to act natural."

My parents did not like my going to the tree house in the first place. Now, with the admiral ensconced, there was the added fear of trigger-happy guards. In fact, the Japanese sailors posted to the house had already discovered me in my roost. One fellow pointed his rifle at me, grinning. I froze, and heard the wings of death flapping by. But the sailor only made a lewd gesture and sauntered off. Soon other guards came to gawk up at me. I pretended to mind my own business, certain they could hear the wild hammering of my heart.

Despite my terror I went back to the tree house the next day, and every day thereafter, impelled by an irresistible force. Eventually I lost my fear, and the Japanese soldiers lost interest in me. One afternoon a lady in a white kimono appeared in the new gazebo. Twirling a parasol gently with her porcelain-pale hand, she stood contemplating the view. When she turned, our eyes met. She smiled and inclined her head; I did the same. Presently she left. The garden suddenly seemed incomplete, even desolate, without her.

THE ADMIRAL ARRIVED a few days later. A tall, spare gentleman with courtly manners, he wore his uniform and medals with an air of weary resignation. I'm sure my presence in the tree house must have registered somewhere behind his expressionless eyes. Though he never gave any sign of being aware of me, the guards were withdrawn from the garden. Soon their numbers were reduced to one at the front gate and another at the rear.

The admiral lived by the clock. Promptly at four-thirty, his charcoal-burning car wheezed up the hill. His wife waited in the gazebo, fanning a brazier, over which sat a smoke-blackened teapot. Bowls were laid out on a low table placed between deep cushions. On another table to one side stood a wind-up gramophone. Beside it was arranged an orderly stack of record albums. Soon the admiral appeared, having changed into an earth-coloured yukata fastened round the waist with a wide black sash. Husband and wife bowed formally, exchanging pleasantries in low voices. He sat cross-legged on one of the cushions, facing the sea and the setting sun while she served tea. After the first cup, the admiral inclined his head towards the gramophone. His wife wound the machine and put on a record. The most wonderful music floated up to the tree house. I too sat facing the westering sun, imitating the man and woman next door, as music wove wild patterns of light and shade against the lids of my closed eyes.

The music did not stop until the sun dipped beneath the horizon. The admiral and his wife sat silently together until the light had faded. After they'd made their way indoors, the orderly noiselessly removed everything from the gazebo. By then it was almost dark; from the tree house, only his white gloves were visible, darting about like nocturnal birds.

Sitting cross-legged in my tree house day after day, I became a vicarious part of this ritual. A wonderful sense of well-being settled over me as the music took its place in my life, the key to a world apart. In a most unlikely way, I had discovered my own magic circle.

BACK IN 1941 the Americans had agreed with the British that if the United States entered the war, the main Allied effort would be concentrated on defeating Germany and Italy. Offensives against Japan would have to follow victory in Europe. No overall plan or agreement was made between the American and British High Commands regarding Japan until the Casablanca conference in January 1943. While the British balked at committing almost a third of the Allied resources to defeating Japan, they did agree that the Americans could go ahead with further offensives against the Japanese. The long-anticipated American offensives in the Pacific got under way in June 1943. The new advance across the central Pacific involved thousands of tiny islands, from the Gilberts, near the equator, north and west through the Marshalls, the Carolinas, and the Marianas. This had long been recognized as the shortest route to Japan; now it was seen as the most advantageous way to deploy American naval and amphibian strength.

The island-hopping war began shakily, with the battle for Tarawa in the Gilbert Islands. The United States suffered enormous casualties, but the campaign proved the efficacy of bypassing and isolating strong garrisons and assaulting weaker ones.

The names of other islands we did not know existed were soon stamped on our consciousness: Majuro and Kwajalein in the Marshalls; Saipan, Tinian, and Guam in the Marianas. The list seemed endless. Each little dot on the map was the scene of unbelievable bloodshed.

Japan's loss of the Marianas in June 1944 had serious repercussions. Japan's inner ring of de-fences had been penetrated. As a result, Tojo's government fell. The islands of Saipan, Tinian, and Guam also put the new American long-range B-29 bomber within reach of the Japanese homeland. Although the press was muzzled, news that Tokyo had been bombed leaked out in China. Father said it was the beginning of the end of the war.

At school we wore our coats in class. The concrete walls and floors were like slabs of ice. The cold crept up through my feet, and after a while the ache spread insidious numbness through my body. The teacher's voice faded in and out, and I felt a terrible need to sleep. We were driven outside with canes to run round the playing field; we could see our feet but couldn't feel them. We were too numb even to feel the cane that drove us on, or the stones that cut into hands and knees when we fell.

One day I fell asleep in class and couldn't be wakened. Father was notified and Lao Zhao came to take me home. I became mortally ill and for days hovered between life and death. Dreams and waking became confused; consciousness was fleeting. Mother was there whenever I opened my eyes, smiling her half-sad smile.

It was spring again before I was well enough to heave myself into my tree house, afraid no one would be next door. As always, the admiral and his wife, in flowing robes, sat with their backs to me, facing the late afternoon sun. Nothing had changed except the music. Instead of rich orchestral sounds, a handful of instruments played, music that was unfamiliar but reassuring, balm for the heart and soul.

AUGUST 6, 1945, was an unusually hot, still day. The sun blazed through a high white haze of extraordinary brilliance. The cicadas whirred and fell silent. Flowers drooped. Even the birds seemed to gasp in the trees, fretful, songless. The air was so dense breathing was an effort.

Father did not go to his office that morning. He had been up most of the night wrestling with the radio transmitter. I could smell his cigar through the cracks of the study door and hear him pacing back and forth. Mother was in her room. The servants remained in their quarters. Only the chickens in their coop went about their usual business.

From the terrace, the sea gleamed, flat and hard as burnished steel. In the naval base, a few ships rode at anchor. Nothing moved. I needed something to shatter the awful stillness; to run about; to yell. But my limbs felt leaden, and some mysterious force smothered my voice.

There was no relief from the oppressive heat even in the tree house. I must have dozed off when the droning of an airplane made me come to with a start. The plane glowed like a jewel against the washed-out sky. The sound, though far off, drew Mother to her window. She called to me to come inside. I pretended not to hear.

"Come inside!" She sounded edgy.

I started down the rope ladder as a trail of tiny dots fell in the plane's wake. "It's all right, Mother. They're only pamphlets."

I was mesmerized. I had a collection of pamphlets hidden in a shoebox under my bed. As the first of the leaflets fluttered down, I let out a whoop and raced about snatching them out of the air. Father came out and picked one up. Mother joined us, and Father translated for her: "Today the atomic bomb was dropped on Hiroshima. The war will soon be over …"

"What does it mean?" she asked anxiously.

"It's the new weapon," Father said, putting a reassuring arm around her.

"What will happen now?"

"Japan will give up," he said.

"Then what?"

Father sighed. "China is her own worst enemy."

In town there was a complete news blackout. People sensed something momentous had happened and kept to their homes until they knew what it was. Meanwhile, Mayor Yue appeared at our door, wan and sweaty and anxious to speak with Father.

"None of us were collaborators," he said in English, for Mother's benefit. "We were agents of the national government in Chung-king. Oh, some of us may have taken advantage of the situation, yes."

"Some people certainly did," said Mother.

"But that was only camouflage."

"That's what you call it?"

"It was for the cause!"

"Was it."

I waited in my tree house that afternoon, but the admiral and his wife failed to appear. There was no movement, no sound from their house. The shadows lengthened across the garden. Still they did not come to the gazebo. Finally Zhang called me in to dinner. I knew the admiral and his wife had gone from my life as mysteriously as they had come.

Later, as I was preparing for bed, the doorbell rang. When Zhang answered, no one was there. Two stacks of record albums had been left outside our gate—the complete symphonies of Beethoven, Haydn, Schubert, Schumann, Tchaikovsky, Brahms. Nearly all the concerti in the popular repertoire. The operas of Wagner, Puccini, and Verdi, as well as a dizzying assortment of chamber music by Beethoven, Brahms, Dvorak, Schumann, Schubert, Haydn, Mendelssohn, and Mozart. Along with the albums was a note in Japanese: "For our young friend in the tree."

Yves Berger, cow-painting

Michael from Yvs 05/93

Bodies in the Basement

RUSSELL BANKS

WHENEVER I happen to meet and talk with people who are complete strangers to me but who know me, insofar as one can, only through my writings, they almost always say that they're surprised (and perhaps relieved) to find that I'm not depressed. And I'm not—neither clinically nor in affect. But I can understand why a stranger, having read my work, might *expect* me to be depressed, at least in affect—that is, withdrawn, down-at-the-mouth, enervated, possibly even surly and curt. In those novels and stories, after all, there are no happy endings; the characters endure lives led mostly in quiet desperation; and on the rare occasions when they do escape from their traps, they tend to do it in ways that only make things worse for themselves and for the people who love them. The comedy, when there is some, is likely to be on the dark side of pessimism and dread; and if at the end there is "redemption," it's only because we have seen that in this material world there is, gratuitously given, *something*, rather than the merely *nothing* we properly deserve. Beyond that, everything the characters both do and don't do seems to derive its final meaning from the overriding fact that nobody gets out of here alive.

But even if I did express through my personality and body the affect that people seem to expect from a depressed person (withdrawn, down-at-the-mouth, enervated, etc.), it would only indicate that my view of the world has made me, not necessarily depressed, but sad and angry. As, indeed, it has. Thus the reader is right to expect to find me sad and angry (if only because the work has made him or her feel that way, too). Which is fine by me, if they feel that way, since I want the novels and stories to be true to my view of the world, and in my view the world is such that any other response to it than sadness and anger would be inappropriate.

Having said that, however, it should also be said that it's precisely the writing of those novels and stories, the act of making them up, that releases me in my day-to-day life and my personal dealings with other people *not* to feel sad and angry. So that, when I push myself away from my desk and rejoin the company of my dear wife, my family and friends, and even the company of strangers, I'm freed to overflow freshly with what feels like a natural sociability and *joie de vivre*, the way a comedian, finished with *his* act, is freed to walk off the stage and let his smile fade, to slump into his chair, look into his dressing room mirror, and place his hands over his face and weep.

For this reason alone—that there exists a sharp distinction between my attitude and my consciousness—no person who is clinically depressed is likely to have written my novels and stories. Of course, no one other than I, depressed or not, could have written them anyhow. My point is simply that, given the nature of the work, I could not possibly be suffering from depression. Fiction, unlike poetry, is not so much a portrait of the author's consciousness as it is a dramatized expression of his attitude. I speak of the difference between fiction and poetry as one who has written fiction for nearly forty years and who began by writing poetry as well and has been married to a practicing poet for over a decade. Beyond that, from my experience of depression, which derives mainly from my continuing happy marriage to the poet just mentioned, a woman who happens to be clinically depressed, scrupulously self-analytical, and supremely articulate, I have come to believe that the consciousness of a depressed person rarely supports an attitude (or fiction) like mine. A depressed fiction-writer with an attitude filled to the brim with sadness and anger nourished, not like mine by an hierarchy of value, but instead by her malfunctioning limbic-diencephalic systems, would probably be suicidal. Unable to separate her consciousness from such an attitude, unable to withdraw from it as the comedian withdraws from his comedy, she would likely be destroyed by it.

A fiction writer's attitude, generally referred to as an author's "vision," is what informs and gives meaning, especially moral meaning, to the plot, the form and structure of the narrative, the point of view, and the characters; it gives meaning even to the tiniest detail, to the sheen, if singled out, reflected off the dewy surface of a single oak leaf at dawn. Everything in a story or novel, by its nature and placement, by the very tone and inflection of the language in which it is borne, reveals, for better or worse, the writer's hierarchy of value. And as

I've implied above, this characteristic of fiction is wonderfully liberating to the writer. Whether he's aware of it is irrelevant. The point is that he is able to distinguish functionally between his work and his personality, which is to say, between the manifestations of his attitude and those of his consciousness. (I might even say, between his body of work and his body.) For him, the two are under no compunction to be the same or even similar. Yet, for the poet, it seems, they are. This, to me, is not just a crucial difference between the poet and the fiction-writer; it is also a crucial difference between a person who is depressed and one who is not. And thus it represents a crucial difference between my wife and me.

WHEN I FIRST came to know and love my wife, I had only a vague and, as it turned out, wrong-headed idea of the true nature of depression. I regarded it more or less the same way as do those readers who—made sad and angry by my work, made "depressed" by it—expect to find me withdrawn, down-at-the-mouth, enervated, etc.. In other words, despite what I knew about my bifurcated self, or selves, I assumed that my wife's personality originated in her attitude, her view of the world, and was therefore pretty much under her control. I saw her personality, her consciousness, as a product of her will, and if there was a down-side, it was the price in easy sociability that, unlike her sociable husband, she, who was clearly tougher than he and more stringently self-sufficient, was willing to pay in order to stay visibly consistent with her views. Which views I took to be characterized by sadness and anger—like mine. Other people might not understand her, but I did.

In fact, there was much about her "affect" (it was far more and other than mere affect, of course, but I didn't realize it yet) that I had not previously associated with depression, but should have, and found seductive, interesting, and energizing. All right, sexy. She was a fast-moving lady, someone who walked up the backs of other people's heels on a crowded sidewalk, with quick, nervy (but not nervous) gestures and sudden shifts of expression and attention, so that all my modes of attention were put on high alert. And to a fellow in middle-age, especially one grown a little jaded and inattentive, high alert can be very exciting. Her insomnia suggested a sensibility more refined than mine, lighter and brighter, and her history of migraines and fear of their return lent drama to stress. Also, her careful hedges against stress, the elaborate ways in which she protected herself against it, simply meant to me that she lived a more stressful life than I, an unfortunate but redeeming consequence, I felt, of her having more *consciousness* than I. Any aspect of her behaviour that she explained as having been caused by depression, I took to be the result of her principled, clear-eyed, realistic view of the world that surrounded us. And her account of having viewed herself since childhood as separated from her true self by a pane of glass, dissociated, yet always self-aware, as if trapped in an infinite regress—this struck me as a slightly heightened and metaphoric way of describing the detachment from one's self that all writers require and actually nourish: I merely thought that she was describing a familiar thing in a new way.

In those early months and well into the first few years of our life together, like all couples newly in love, we told each other the stories of our past marriages and love affairs and our complex, often painful relations with our parents, siblings, and, in my case, children. Like most such couples, we were better able to describe our lows than our highs, or perhaps felt freer to linger over unhappiness and dissatisfaction than their opposites, and emphasized traumatic disruption over easy, inevitable maturation, growth, and change. We described our difficult childhoods, our tormented adolescences, our past loves (in particular the ones we regretted and had suffered from), and our up-to-now neglected emotional, spiritual, and sexual needs: we told each other about the bodies buried in our basements. And in so doing, discovered that we were perfect for each other.

Time passed, and slowly, as in any marriage, a third person, who was neither of us, began to join us in our marriage, a person smiling beneficently between us, with an invisible arm draped across our shoulders. It was a person whose identity participated in both our separate identities and was, without our intending it or knowing how it happened, our mutual creation, containing both genders, both pasts, both personalities—someone utterly trusted in whom we each could see him- or herself *and* the other, but could see neither one nor the other alone. This third person, whose identity feels more real than one's own, makes a marriage

transcendent, but also, when one or both the partners fail the marriage, makes divorce so difficult to endure, living on, as it must, for years after the marriage has been dissolved, keeping ex-husband and ex-wife from knowing who they are alone, what they like and dislike independently of the other, and what their own secret stories were and are. It's not unlike the invisible third person who appears in one's family when a parent or sibling or child is an addict or alcoholic and whose presence alters everyone's behaviour and perceptions in tiny, incremental ways, until before long everyone in the family has changed to such a degree that no one, not even the addict, can know who he is anymore or who the others are without that third person present. It's how one becomes an "enabler." But in a marriage that's not organized around addiction or alcoholism, it's how one becomes a usefully sympathetic and understanding spouse.

In marriage we put our identities at risk, gambling that change will turn out to be improvement. I can't speak for my wife, but in my case, change has been improvement—at least insofar as I came over time to feel, not quite her pain, but her depression. And gradually came to realize that I'd had it all wrong.

I BEGAN TO SUSPECT that I might have a few things wrong when I came to the surprising conclusion that, for the first time in my life, I was feeling, not sad and angry, not even melancholic or gloomy, but depressed. I was manifesting certain classic symptoms—small phobias, along with elaborately contrived avoidances, and the sort of distraction one associates with anxiety, especially the anxiety that arises from fear of losing control over every aspect of one's life. Also, minor sleep disorder and the anxiety that creates. I had never before asked myself, on waking in the morning, if I'd had a good or bad night's sleep, but now it was a regular morning interrogatory, a ruthless, irritated demand for an answer. And I was acquiring a new and noticeable (to me) detachment from myself, an alienation from the person who spoke and acted for me—an unwanted, counter-productive extension of the familiar and necessary detachment I'd long maintained from the man with my name who composed, with attitude, my novels and stories.

The phobias first, for they appeared first and were the tip-off. For years, certainly since her adolescence, my wife had suffered from what we half-jokingly called "urbophobia," fear of cities, especially New York City, an *urb* I rather loved, had visited all my life, and had resided in from 1982 until 1988, the year my wife and I set up housekeeping together in Princeton, New Jersey, where I was then teaching. Since my adolescence, I had responded to Gotham pretty much the way small-town American intellectuals have reacted since Whitman's time, romanticizing its history like Thomas Wolfe, glamourizing its funky bohemianism like Kerouac, and embracing its varieties of humanity like a social scientist on speed. Everything about the city excited me and nourished my mind; nothing repelled or scared me (although, naturally, I avoided danger with the same rational care that I took when crossing streets against the lights—I always looked both ways).

Until, having failed to displace my wife's phobia with my enthusiasm for the city, I began to see it with her eyes, instead of my own. The city hadn't changed; I had. Now it seemed physically and psychically threatening to me, noisy and invasive, chaotic and cruel; for the first time, I found myself judging my numerous friends who continued to love the city as I once had, viewing them as somehow more parochial than I and sentimental and self-deluded. None of this, of course, was my wife's doing, none of it was her desire. Quite the opposite. She felt embarrassed by her fear of the city, handicapped by it, and the last thing she wanted was to share that fear with me. Yet there it was: in looking out for her, I had begun to look out *with* her. Failing to protect her from a thing she feared, I had come to fear it myself.

It was the same with all but a few of her other symptoms of depression. Although I never suffered from migraines, I worried that perhaps I would, or should, and although I never slipped into the slough of near-suicidal despond that she sometimes endured, I began to magnify my own occasional dips and slips into morbidity and to rely less on humour to get me back on track and more on anxiety and agitated will, which, predictably, got focussed on issues and occasions of control: the more I felt able to control matters both large and small, the less likely the fall into despondency. It was a mildly effective solution, but the end result was a raised level of ongoing anxiety and the constant care and feeding of a fast-growing control-freak.

My reaction to all this was to blame my wife—to be angry at her, first, for not having allowed me to cure her of her depression, and then for infecting me with it. Crude, I know, but not uncommon, I fear (especially among custodial males with the bodies of failed fathers buried beneath their basement floors). Happily, it didn't take long for me to see that my wife was not responsible for my condition. I was. Physician, I told myself, cure thyself, and saw then that this self-inflicted "infection" was in fact a homeopathic cure, in which like cures like and by means of which I was allowed to see the extreme and defining difference between my minor case of depression, contracted by my having confused empathy with sympathy, and my wife's major case, which went, not with her choice of spouse or diet or job or residence, but with her brain chemistry. It went with her body. And bodies don't have attitudes; they have consciousness.

In the intervening years, much has changed, and all for the better, partly because of my growing comprehension of the nature and etiology of my wife's condition, but mostly because of the rapid development and deployment of anti-depressants. In the meantime, I have learned a great moral lesson and have tried to apply it to as many aspects of my life with my wife and others, even strangers, as possible. I have learned to feel *for* my wife and to avoid feeling *with* her, and to avoid feeling for other people and not with them. To sympathize and not empathize. It now seems clear to me that it is arrogant for me to claim to feel another person's pain—unless I'm willing to *become* that person. A fiction writer can do that with his characters. And perhaps, if he wishes to write fiction that will matter to strangers, he must do that. But a husband cannot become his own wife. Not if he wants to go on loving her in sickness and in health; not if he wants her to love him back.

Jacqueline Rau, *Nature Morte*, 1930

The White Monk

MARY MORRIS

ALMOST ALL WE COULD SEE was the castle. It loomed on a hillside above our apartment in Prague. In fact it was not the castle I had expected. I had thought it would be a real castle with turrets and ramparts, fortified walls. This was more like a small village on a hill.

I had come to Prague to teach a class and also to study. I was going to learn about Jewish Prague and Kafka was a piece of this. I had signed up to take a class on the golem, being taught by writer and scholar Rodger Kamenetz. I was to be in Prague for a week before my husband arrived, to get my bearings. In the golem class I learned that the golem was a creature made out of mud from the banks of the Vltava. That Rabbi Loew was supposed to have made him to save the Jewish people. That a golem is a creature made to protect or serve a master but who soon is out of control. There are many golem stories, Frankenstein being the most well-known, but the myth originated here in Prague and I felt it was part of my understanding of the city we were living in for a month, as well as my desire to know more about Eastern European Jewish history, to have an understanding of the golem.

THE DAY L. ARRIVED it began to rain. I thought it would be a brief shower as my first rain in Prague had been, but in fact it didn't stop. It had been my plan as soon as L. arrived to take him up to the castle, for I had not been and my teaching schedule did not permit it. The funicular was reputed to be near our house. I had not seen it, but I knew we could take the funicular up to Petrin Hill, then walk along the wall of Hunger, named because the poor people of Prague who built it were starving and built the wall to pay for their food.

Havel lived in the castle and Kafka himself had used a tiny house as a studio on a road called the Golden Lane. But it rained all day when L. arrived. It rained all day Saturday and then Sunday. Every time we checked the Prague weather on the Internet it showed days of rain and then the sun, but as we approached the day when the sun was to appear it had again receded into showers and so the sun, like the castle, eluded us.

On rainy afternoons instead of going to the castle, I sat in an armchair and read *The Castle*. I had become interested in Kafka over the years in part because he is writer who turned to his Jewish roots late in his life. What surprised me most was how much it resembled K.'s castle in the Kafka novel by the same title. "On the whole the Castle, as it appeared from this distance, corresponded to K.'s expectations. It was neither an old knight's fortress nor a magnificent new edifice, but a large complex, made up of a few two-story buildings and many lower, tightly packaged ones; had one not known that this was a castle, one could have taken it for a small town."

Kafka scholars have long disputed which castle Kafka meant. Since he spent much of his later years in sanitoriums in villages that had castles, many have speculated that it was one of these he is referring to in his novel. But as I read his book, staring at the castle on the hillside ahead of me, I felt certain that he must have meant this one, the one he had spent his childhood gazing at and that had somehow eluded him, as most things had.

ON SUNDAY despite the rain we took the tour of Jewish Prague. We met across from the Franz Kafka Café in front of the Precious Legacy Tour company. We were told to look for the giant statue of the golem, serving tea. The Jewish Museum in Prague consists of five synagogues, all of which contain Jewish artifacts. It had been Hitler's intention to turn Prague into a museum of Jewish life. Once the Jews were exterminated, then Prague and its magnificent synagogues and the artifacts that Jewish families had left behind would serve as an educational reminder of Jewish culture and life.

On the walls of Pinkus synagogue are inscribed the names of the Jews of Bohemia and Moravia who were exterminated by the Nazis. Some 77,000 names appear on the wall, including those of Franz Kafka's three sisters and their families. Had Kafka lived, his life too would have ended here. It is often said that his writing was prescient; that the themes of *The Trial* and *The Castle* reflect the pointless tyranny of Nazism to come.

In Prague I was also reading the memoir by Helen Epstein, entitled *Where She Came From: A Daughter's Search for Her Mother's History.* I came to see how Kafkaesque the life of the Jews in Prague became. As Nazi rules hemmed them in, they were only allowed to shop at certain hours. They could not go into parks, playgrounds, or on boats. They could not go to movies, theatres, or buy newspapers. They had to turn in their radios and typewriters. They could not own pets. They could not buy apples.

It is as if the penal colony—when the crime you are accused of is being written on your chest and you will not know what the crime is until it has been written and by then you are dead—came to life.

EVERY DAY when I was not working and we were not studying the golem and the history of Jewish Prague, we tried to get to the castle. We'd set off, thinking the weather would clear, but then the rains came down. Finally after a week we got a break in the weather and we headed out. We thought the funicular was to the left of where we were living, but in fact it was to the right. We took it to the top and began to walk towards the castle.

We followed the road along the Hunger Wall, then decided it wasn't the right way and it was taking us away from the castle. There was a small opening in the wall that seemed to lead to a path, and I told L. that perhaps we were just on a road that was taking us around the city. That we were somehow outside the castle when we in fact needed to be inside. L. agreed that it looked as if we were on a service road that was not going to lead to the castle. He wanted to go to the bludiste, a maze made up of mirrors, but I often felt disoriented in mazes, which I suppose is the point, and one made up of mirrors seemed as if it would be more disorienting. So we agreed to go through the opening in the Hunger Wall and follow it to the castle.

The opening was the size of a small door and lead to a dirt path. The path went into a kind of open field, but we could see nothing more of the castle than we had been able to see from the other side of the wall. In fact now we could not see the castle at all and it seemed as if it no longer existed , just a figment of our imaginations, not a real place we had looked at for days on end in the gray, rainy weather, or as the sun peeked through the clouds, a place that seemed full of promise, but now had all but disappeared.

We continued along this path, but soon the path became overgrown and the wall crumbly and this did not seem to be the right way at all. We crawled through an opening in the wall back into the service road we had been on. We followed it until the end when we came into a street and a cobblestone plaza. We looked in our guidebook to see where we were but couldn't seem to make sense out of it.

At last we looked into the walled city and saw the Strahov Monastery which I recalled as having an excellent library and that this was also on the way to the castle.

THE CASES THAT LINED the front of the library rooms contained the odd, desiccated bodies of sea creatures. Giant lobsters, the skin of a huge snake, the shells of giant turtles, dried up stingrays, weird fish, an array of butterflies and beetles, narwhal and elephant tusks, rhinoceros horns, and one sea creature which appeared to be a fish with wings, more mythological than real.

We were not allowed inside the library itself. Instead we had to stand behind a rope and gaze at the room, lined floor to ceiling with collection of eighteenth century books, the globes, inlaid wood rotating reading tables. I have a passion for globes, especially old globes. I love to see what the world looked like three hundred years ago and I like to spin them and imagine people planning journeys, based on these strange maps of the world.

The rope at the first room was crowded with tourists but the second room we noticed further down, was not. We were admiring the second room of books when I noticed the white monk approaching. He was dressed entirely in long white robes. His head had been shaved and he wore wire-rimmed glasses and a slightly bemused look on his face. He was followed by two men in blue jeans and jackets who appeared to be a gay couple.

The white monk reached for the rope that kept us from going inside the library and let the two men pass. Then he closed it as he entered the library with them. I stood by the rope with L. hanging back, listening as the white monk spoke in a gentle, soothing voice in very broken English, telling the two men about the globes which he let them spin. He turned the rotating reading table and demonstrated how one could read many books at once. I saw the men, leaning forward, listening to every word the white monk said, and I tried to make out his words but he was leaning close to the men and his speech was garbled.

We were hungry when we left the library and Hell was right around the corner. Literally, it was a restaurant named Pelko which means hell, built in an old wine cellar, damp, lit in red, and pointlessly expensive. So we went to Hell and there I told L. that I wanted to have the white monk show me the library. He said he did too. He had seen in the guidebook where tours of the Strahov Library could be arranged in advance and I told him that this was what I wanted and be sure to tell them we want the white monk.

The next day L. tried to phone. He phoned several times. There was no answering machine and when someone did answer, they only spoke Czech and usually hung up. "Maybe the guidebook doesn't give the right number," I said. L., seeing that I was dejected and wanting to go into the library itself, phoned once more and this time a person answered. "Do you speak English?" he asked. The person he had on the phone did not speak English but it seemed that the next person he spoke with did and that L. was able to arrange with several back and forth a tour for us at two o'clock the following Thursday.

SINCE THURSDAY was two days away and I had a free day we decided to make a day trip to Terezin. I had never been to a concentration camp before and didn't really want to go, but I had promised a friend back home that I would see it. He said I could not understand what it meant to be a Jew in Eastern Europe if I did not go to Terezin.

The buses left every twenty minutes and our bus was filled with Czechs, Israelis, a couple from Spain with their child. We drove through the rolling hills of Bohemia until we came to what was clearly a fortress. It had a moat around it and on the lawn in front of it a tall Jewish star stood beside a cross. But the bus did not stop at the fortress, even though an elderly Israeli couple had asked the driver if they could get off. In fact there was no stop near the fortress at all.

The bus kept going a mile or so into town. In town we stopped at the tourist information office where the clerk told us that the fortress was just for political prisoners. When I pressed her, regarding the Jewish star on the lawn, she said "there is a cross there."

"And a star."

"I don't know," the woman replied, "but it was only for political prisoners."

The town itself had been the ghetto, the model concentration camp where children went to school and adults put on operas until after the Red Cross visited and they were shipped off to Auschwitz and Dachau. Twelve thousand Jewish children were sent to Terezin. Two hundred returned.

Beyond its strange history, the town was oddly dreary. We walked, map in hand, along cracked sidewalks, through town squares, littered with garbage, the grass overgrown. Beneath the trees were only muddy patches of lawn. As we approached the small fortress, as it is known, the star and the cross loomed on the lawn where they marked the mass graves of "political prisoners."

Inside the prison we examined the tiny, windowless rooms where fourteen or more men lived, saw the museum that outlined the deportation of Jews to Terezin, read entries in the guestbook such as those from two granddaughters whose grandmother had perished at Auschwitz. We passed rooms where men had been shackled to the walls and tortured to death, stood at the spot where the French poet and resistance fighter, Robert Desnos, was killed in the last days of the war.

Then L. and I looked at one another. I could not look into another windowless cell, another tiny room with manacles on the wall. There were two buses back to Prague. We opted for the early one.

OVER DINNER we told a friend of our difficulties in reaching the castle and said that we had arranged a tour of the Strahov Library and wanted to be sure to arrive on time. She informed us that the #22 tram, which was the one I took every day to go to school, went right there and it was the most direct way to arrive at the castle. "You just have to stay on the tram," she said, "And you can't miss it."

The next day on the #22 tram I didn't see a stop for the monastery. I asked a Czech woman for Strahov Monastery and she pointed to Malovanka. As we wound up along a hill, past the wall of the castle, Malovanka was further than seemed right, but we went all that way. When we got off in a residential neighbourhood, the monastery was nowhere to be seen. After several attempted phone calls to explain that we would be late for our two o'clock tour, a pedestrian pointed the way.

In fact the Strahov Monastery was only a few hundred yards from where the tram had let us off, though we could not see it from where we stood. But when we arrived, the ticket sales person did not know anything about a tour and did not speak English so I asked the ticket taker. She was a large Czech woman who wore a wool cardigan on a warm summer's day. I pointed to the page in the guidebook and said we had a tour, arranged with the monks. She nodded, seeming to know what I was speaking about and took us outside. She pointed to a gate that was padlocked shut on the side of the monastery.

Behind the gate was a grassy path that led to nowhere. I looked at the padlocked gate and she pointed once again in that direction. I shrugged my arms, surprised and she shooed me that way. To convince her that I could not go through this gate I went over and shook it. She pointed to another door this one smaller, wooden and I shook that as well. Then she made a big circle with her arms, indicating that the way to go was all the way around the monastery.

L. looked at me and shrugged. Perhaps we decided there was an administrative office where the white monk waits for his tour and that we would find it on the other side of the church. But after walking almost all the way around the monastery we saw that it was useless. We returned to the library and went upstairs to the gift shop where the woman spoke English. "Oh, she sent you the wrong way. You must go all the way to the other side and she made a big sweep of her arms, a circle as the Czech woman had done only this time going the opposite way. Relieved, we thanked her, feeling closer to our goal.

As I felt us nearing the goal of the white monk who would take us within the confines of the library, I turned to L. and said, "The first time you are just finding your way; the second time you are actually going there." He shrugged again and nodded as we followed the foot path that led to a wall and a gate with a door. The door was ajar and without hesitating I wandered in.

We found ourselves in a small courtyard and just ahead of us was what appeared to be a building with offices. Making our way inside, we wandered along the long corridor of offices without windows. A woman stood behind the glass doors of what appeared to be a research library, keys in her hands, refusing to acknowledge our presence in any way.

Then a man appeared from behind a door. "Are you tourists?" he asked. I told him no. That we had come for a guided tour with the white monk. He looked at me strangely, then disappeared behind another door. This time a woman appeared. She was young and thin, with a scholarly air. She informed us in very bad English that she would give us a tour the following Monday but she could not give us a tour on that day. I told her we would be gone the next week and she said she was sorry.

I didn't want her anyway, I told L. as we left the administrative offices. I wanted the white monk in

his ghostly apparel to show us the books and the globes and explain the desiccated animal that looked like a bird/fish. As we stood in the sun in the courtyard, I noticed a large man who had come out of a guardhouse, just across from us.

He was huge, dressed in a blue uniform. His face was square, his jaw set, and he stared at us in silence. A car was parked in front of the guard house and on its door I read, "Golem Security Forces." We looked up and the man was now joined by another, who looked and stood, arms across his chest, just like his companion.

Without a word, L. and I made our way to the door through which we'd come. As we exited, it was slammed behind us. I turned and saw the sign, "Privat," on the door.

As L. and I walked down from the castle, we saw the signs for the Golden Lane. This was where Kafka had once had a studio and we followed the signs until we came to a street of tiny cottages, painted in bright shades of blue and yellow, lime green and rose. It looked as if elves might live there. Kafka had written such stories as "A Country Doctor" in this studio. All the cottages had been turned into souvenir and craft stores. I noticed that Kafka's studio was #22, the same number as the tram that had brought us here. His studio had been turned into a shop for postcards and memorabilia. We purchased a few postcards, mainly scenes of Prague and the Jewish cemetery before making our way home.

An introduction to

"The Sealion Hunter"

ROBERT BRINGHURST

GHANDL of the Qayahl LLaanas was a Haida speaking mythteller, born around 1851 in the Haida village of Qaysun, "Sealion Town." It is an empty beachfront now, but it was home, in the early nineteenth century, to three hundred people or more, and it was then only one of some forty big villages peppering the thousand-mile coast of an archipelago known as Xhaaydla Gwaayaay. No such places are now listed in official gazetteers. Qaysun is an unmarked spot near the northwest corner of an island known as Moresby, in a cluster of islands mapped as the Queen Charlottes and locally known as Haida Gwaii, south of the southern tip of Alaska and west of the British Columbia mainland. On the map and in the tax collector's ledgers, these islands are a part of Canada, the Commonwealth of Nations and the continent of North America. Ghandl did not know or use these names. He knew instead the land, the plants, the animals of the islands, the speech of his own people, and the ever-present, ever-changing sea. Qaysun is on the edge of the continental shelf, facing seven thousand miles of open ocean.

It was at Hlghagilda (now Skidegate), in November 1900, that Ghandl dictated the texts I have translated as *Nine Visits to the Mythworld*. John Reed Swanton, a linguist, commissioned him to tell the stories and hired another Haida, Henry Moody, to serve as the principal listener. Ghandl dictated, usually six hours a day, six days a week, for roughly three weeks. Moody repeated his words sentence by sentence, hour by hour, and Swanton wrote them down in laborious but usually quite accurate phonetics. Early the next year, Swanton and Moody went over the transcripts word by word to make a literal interlinear translation. Those interlinear translations would be very welcome now, as the best record of how Henry Moody understood what Ghandl said. But after Swanton used these interlinears, in 1902-3, to make his running prose translation, he apparently destroyed them. What we have to work with now are the Haida texts as Swanton typed them, in Washington DC, in 1902, and his English prose translations.

Tradition is important in Native American cultures, as it is in every functioning culture, but the major works of Native American literature are major works of art, and the makers of these works are every bit as individual as any artists anywhere. It seems to me quite wrong to describe such works as "folklore" or as "Indian legends." They are never, at root, anonymous. Nor are they works of corporate authorship, mindlessly recited by nameless, faceless agents of the tribe. If Ghandl's poems are folk tales, then the paintings of Andrea Mantegna are folk art and the sonatas of Franz Schubert are folk music. None of these works could come to be without the force of a living tradition, but none of them is the fruit of tradition alone.

Erna Gunther, a respected and respectful anthropologist, worked for many years among the Coast Salish peoples of Puget Sound, a thousand miles south of Haida Gwaii. In 1925, she published *Klallam Tales*, an anthology of stories told to her in the Klallam language—but the stories were interpreted on the spot by a multilingual colleague and written down in English only. Gunther makes a point of naming the narrator of each story, but she did not record as Swanton did, any narrator's actual words. Gunther presupposed—correctly, I am sure—that stories told by Klallam individuals could give her a kind of insight into the mind of the Klallam nation as a whole. But I am puzzled by another of her assumptions—one widely shared by

some in the present day. Gunther says in the introduction to her book that "One of the problems in the study of oral literature is the influence of the narrator on the literary style of the story."

I imagine that by reading French or Russian novels I can learn quite a bit about the mind of the French or Russian nation. It would not, however, usually occur to me to say that one of the *problems* in the study of written literature is the influence of the writer. The effect of the narrator on the story is a problem in the same sense that the hinges are a problem for the door.

Are individuals in cultures that are literate always predisposed to undervalue those in cultures that are oral? I do not know. I know however that the habit can be broken and the prejudice unlearned. Jeremiah Curtin, who died in 1906, was one of the earliest outsiders to make a serious study of Native American oral literature. Curtin understood quite well the vital role of individual creativity in the work of Seneca, Wintu, Yana and Kiksht-speaking mythtellers he knew. Edward Sapir, who began serious work with Native American texts in the same year Curtin died, registered his own enlightenment on this point a few years later, in a tribute to Saayaacchapis, his old Nuuchahnulth teacher. Melville Jacobs made a similar discovery working with Sahaptin, Kiksht, Hanis, and Miluk speakers in the 1920s and early 1930s. Other writers have experienced equal revelations through contact with other oral cultures elsewhere in the world. Marcel Griaule's account of what he learned in Africa in 1946 from his Dogon tutor Ogotemmêli, and Victor Turner's vivid portrait of

Muchona, his Ndembu teacher, are two notable examples.

Ghandl is not here now to show us all, in person, how an individual talent interacts with the tradition in an oral culture, but it is also possible to learn this lesson less directly, through the study and comparison of artefacts or texts. Bill Reid, who taught me much of what I know of Haida art, was intensely aware of the identities of carvers who had died before he was born. He knew the older masters through their works, although he never knew their names. Dell Hymes's detailed studies of Native American texts, conducted over nearly half a century, point strongly in the same direction. When we study Native American art *as art* and Native American literature *as literature*, this is where we head. We learn that the insights and the styles of individual human beings are essential to the symbiotic life of the tradition. Then we can accept them as a treasure, not a problem.

That spark of recognition is dimmed, if not extinquished, where the works are not transcribed in the mythteller's actual language. The major literary works in nearly every Native American language are now apparently condemned to a life lived mostly in translation. But translation that is too quick and easy strips the other's otherness away. And when you take the other's otherness away, the other's sameness and humanity go too.

Like Shakespeare's plays or Rembrant's paintings, Ghandl's poems reach far beyond the world in which their maker lived, yet they never lose their touch with the environment he knew. Ghandl makes the story quintessentially Haida at the same time that he makes it his alone. He roots it in the heart and in the ground that is his home. That is how he makes it human, and thereby universally germane.

The Sealion Hunter

by Ghandl of the Qayahl Llaanas
Translated by Robert Bringhurst

A MASTER CARVER HAD FATHERED
                two children, they say.

They saw game on the reefs,
so he made the harpoon.
He bound it with cord, they tell me.
He used something strong for this purpose, they say.
And he put a detachable barb on the shaft.

They herded the sealions into a pool on top of a reef,
and he was the one who harpooned them.
One thrust, and he pulled out the shaft
and fastened another barb on the end.
This is the way he killed sealions, they say.

When he had been doing this for a while,
they paddled out early one day
and they put him ashore on the reef.
Then they pushed off
and left him.

His wife's youngest brother turned toward him.
There in the midst of the crew, he tugged at their
                                        paddles.
He struggled against them.

The hunter was watching.
He called them again and again.
They paid no attention.

They were unable to kill the sealions.
He was the only one who could do it.
That is the reason they left him, they say.

Alone on the top of the rock, he wept for his children.
He wept for a while,
and then he lay down by the pool.

After he lay there in silence awhile,
something said to him,
<<A headman asks you in.>>

He looked around him.
Nothing stood out,
but he noticed that, there in the pool, something
                                          went under.

When he had lain there a little while longer,
something said the same thing again.
Then, they say, he peeked through the eye
of the marten-skin cape he was wearing.
Then he saw a pied bill grebe break the surface of the
                                                     pool.

After swimming there awhile,
it said, <<A headman asks you in,>>
and then it went under.

HE WRAPPED his fingers round the whetstone
that he wore around his neck,

and he leaped into the pool, they say.

He found himself in front of a large house,
and they invited him inside.
He went in,
and there they asked him,
<<Why is it you are murdering so many of my
                                          women?>>

He answered,
<<I have done what I have done
in order to give food to my two children.>>

In a pool in a corner of the house,
he saw two baby killer whales spouting.
Those, they say, were the headman's children, playing.
In all four corners of the house, he saw
              the dorsal fins of killer whales
hanging up in bunches.

Then, however, they offered him food.
There was a sealion sitting near the door.
They dragged it to the center.

They lifted the cooking rocks out of the fire
and dropped them down its throat.
They dropped a halibut down the throat of the
                                          sealion too.
When the halibut was cooked, they say,
they set it there before him.

When the meal was over,
they brought one of the fins down from the corner.
They heated the base of the fin.

When they made him bend over,
he slung the whetstone around so it hung down his
                                                       back.
When they tried to fasten the fin to his spine,
it fell off.
The fin lay on the stone floorplanks, quivering.

They went to get another.
They heated that one also, right away,
and they forced him to bend over.

Again he moved the whetstone.
When they tried to fasten the fin to his spine,
it fell off like the other,
and it dropped onto the stone floor of the house.

Then they got another.
When the same thing happened yet again,
they went and got a tall one.

After they had warmed it there awhile,
they forced him to bend over once again.
He moved the whetstone round again.
When they tried to fasten that one to his spine,
it too fell shuddering on the stone floor of the house.

After they had tried four times,
they gave it up.
<<Let him go,>> the headman said.
<<He refuses the fin.
Put him into a sealion's belly.>>

Then the headman told him what to do.
<<After you have drifted here and there awhile,

and after you have washed ashore four times,
let yourself out.
You will find that you have come to a fine country.>>

They put him into a sealion's paunch right away.
He sewed it shut from the inside,
and they set him adrift.

WHEN he had floated on the ocean for a while
and washed ashore for the fourth time,
he crawled out.
He had drifted ashore on a sandy beach.

He sewed the paunch up tight from the outside,
and he put it in the water.
It faced upwind
and disappeared to seaward.

Then he walked in the direction of the village.
He waited until nightfall on the outskirts of the town.
After dark, he peeked in at his wife.

His wife had singed her hair off.
He saw soot stains on her face.
He saw that both his children sat there too.

He tapped against the wall just opposite his wife.
She came outside.
He said to her, <<Bring me my tools.>>

She brought him what he asked for.
<<Don't tell anyone I'm here,>> he said.
<<Don't even tell the children.>>

When he left that place,
he grabbed another of the children who were playing
                                                    there.
He took the child up the hill.

AFTER walking for a while,
he came to a big lake.
There was a tall redcedar standing on the shore.

He cut the trunk across the front.
When he made another cut across the back,
the cedar dropped across the surface of the water.

He split it from the butt end.
After splitting it part way,
he braced it open.

Then he stripped and twisted cedar limbs,
splicing them together to make line.
When the line was long enough,
he tied the child to one end.
Then he lowered it into the lake
                between the split halves of the tree.

After letting it touch bottom,
he jigged with it awhile.
Then the line began to jerk,
and he began to haul it in.
By then the lake was boiling.

Its forepaws broke the surface first.
When its head broke the surface just behind them,
he sprang the trap by kicking out the brace.

The creature thrashed and struggled.
He clubbed it again and again,
until he had killed it.

Then he pulled it from the trap.
He touched his knifepoint to its throat,
but then a lightning bolt exploded,
so he started his cut instead from the base of the tail.

He skinned it.
He liked the way its tail looked especially.
It was curled.

Then he built a fire,
and he dried and tanned the skin.
It was a Seawolf that he caught, they say.

After he had tanned it,
he rolled it up
and packed it back to town.

On the outskirts of town stood a hollow redcedar.
He hid it in there.
He put moss over top of it.

THEN he walked away from the edge of the village.
He carved redcedar into the forms of killer whales.
He fitted them with dorsal fins
and pushed them under water with his feet and let
                                                    them go.

Just out beyond low tide mark, some bubbles rose.
Then he said, <<You're on your own.
Go wherever you can live.>>

Those are harbor porpoises, they say.

Next he carved some western hemlock
              into the forms of killer whales.
When he had ten of them,
he pushed them under water with his feet and let
                                        them go.

After they had left,
bubbles rose a little farther seaward.
After that he turned it over in his mind.

Then he said, <<You're on your own.
Go wherever you can live.>>
Those are Dall's porpoises, they say.

All this time, the weather was good, they say,
and as long as it lasted, the men were out fishing.

ON THE FOLLOWING DAY, after thinking again
about what he would use,
he made ten killer whales out of yew wood.

Their skins were shiny black and splashed with white,
their underbellies white,
and they had white patches up behind their mouths.

The dorsal fin of one was nicked along the fore edge.
The dorsal fin of one hooked backward toward the tail.
As he was making them, they moved.

He laid down skids for them to rest on.
Then he launched them,
and he pushed them with his feet to deeper water.

Bubbles rose a long time later, out at sea.

Then he called them in
and hauled them up on shore.
They had snapper, salmon and halibut in their jaws.

EVENING came again,
and he went to see his wife.
Once again he peeked inside,
and then he tapped on the wall beside his wife.
She came outside.

He said to her, <<Tell your youngest brother
he ought to wear a feather in his hair
when the men go fishing in the morning.>>

Next day, when they were fishing,
he gave the killer whales their instructions.
<<Do away with all the humans who are fishing.
Rub your fins on their canoes,
and only save the one who wears a feather in his
                                        hair.>>

Then he nudged them to sea with his feet, they say.
Bubbles rose a while later,
seaward of where the canoes were riding at anchor.

Then the killer whales closed in on the canoes.
Bubbles rose among the boats.
The killer whales rubbed against them with their fins
and chewed the canoes and humans to pieces.
Only one, who wore a feather in his hair, continued
                                        swimming.

When the whales had destroyed them all,
the one who wore a feather in his hair
          climbed aboard a chewed canoe,
and the pod of whales brought him to the shore.
They left him on the beach in front of town.

THEN he called the killer whales again.
He told them what to do.

He said to one who had a knothole in his fin,
<<Pierced Fin will be your name.>>
To one whose fin was wavy, he said,
<<Your name will be Rippled Fin.>>

Then he told them this:
<<Go to House Point.
Make your homes there.
That is a fine country.
People of the Strait will be your name.>>

Then he went to see his wife
with fish the killer whales had brought him in their
                                        mouths.
Both of his children were happy to see him.

WHEN he had been in the village awhile,
he went outside
while others were still sleeping.

He dressed in the Seawolf skin.
There at the edge of the village, he reached out
          and touched the water with one paw,
and he had half of a spring salmon.

His mother-in-law, who nagged him all the time,
always got up early in the morning.
He laid the salmon down at the door of her house.

Early in the morning, she came out.
She found the chunk of salmon
and was happy.

That night again, he dressed in the Seawolf skin.
He went into the water up to the elbow.
He came back with half a halibut.

He set it down beside his mother-in-law's door.
She found it in the morning.
The people of the village had been hungry up till then,
                                        they say.

Again that night, he dressed in the skin of the
                                        Seawolf.
He put his foreleg all the way into the water,
and he got a whole spring salmon.
He set it at the woman's door as well,
and she found it in the morning.

He dressed again the next night in the Seawolf skin,
and then he let the water come over his back.
He brought in the jaw of a humpback whale
and left it at his mother-in-law's door.
She was very pleased to find it there.

HIS MOTHER-IN-LAW started to perform
as a shaman then, they say.
They fasted side by side with her for four nights.
He was with them too, they say.

It was his voice that started speaking through her —
through the mother of his wife.

The next night again, he got inside the Seawolf.
He swam seaward.
He killed a humpback whale.
Fangs stuck out of the nostrils of the Seawolf.
Those are what he killed it with, they say.

He put it up between his ears
and carried it to shore.
He put it down in front of the house.
She had predicted
that a whale would appear.

And again, as they were sleeping,
he went out inside the Seawolf.
He got a pair of humpback whales.

He brought them back to shore.
He carried one between his ears
and the other draped across the base of his tail.
He swam ashore with them
and set them down again in front of the house.

When night came again,
he swam way out to sea inside the Seawolf.
He got ten humpback whales.

He carried several bundled up between his ears.
He carried others in a bunch at the base of his tail.
He had them piled on his body,
and he put one in his mouth.
He started swimming toward the shore.

He was still out at sea when daylight came, they say,
and when he came up on the beach,
the mother of his wife was there to meet him
in the headdress of a shaman.

He stepped outside the Seawolf skin.
<<Why,>> he asked her, <<are there spearpoints in
                                        your eyes?
Does the spirit being speaking through you
get some help from me?>>
She died of shame from what he said, they say.

THE SEAWOLF SKIN swam out to sea alone.
Then the hunter took the string of whales
and said that no one was to touch them.

The sale of those whales made him rich, they say.
And then he held ten feasts in honor, so they say,
        of the youngest brother of his wife.
He made a prince of him.

This is where it ends.

Al Purdy

1918–2000

MICHAEL ONDAATJE

WE WERE VERY YOUNG and he was hitting his stride—*Poems for all the Annettes, The Cariboo Horses*.

There had been no poetry like it yet in this country. Souster and Acorn were similar, had prepared the way, but here was also a voice—with this "strolling" not "dancing" gait or metre, climbing over old fences in Cashel township . . . (And who ever wrote about "township lines" in poems before Al did?)

And with this art of walking he covered greater distances, more haphazardly, and with more intricacy. Cashel and Ameliasburg and Elzevir and Weslemkoon are names we can now put on a literary map alongside the Mississippi and The Strand. For a person of my generation, Al Purdy's poems mapped and named the landscape of Ontario, just as Leonard Cohen did with Montreal and its surroundings in *The Favourite Game*.

We were in our twenties (and I speak for my friends Tom Marshall and David Helwig who were there with me) and we didn't have a single book to our names; we were studying or teaching at Queen's University in Kingston. . . . And Al and Eurithe simply invited us in. And why? Because we were poets! Not well-known writers or newspaper celebrities.

I mean did Kipling ever do that? Did D.H. Lawrence? Malcolm Lowry had done that for "Al—something or other" in Dollarton, years earlier. These visits became essential to our lives. We weren't there for gossip, certainly not to discuss royalties and publishers. We were there to talk about poetry. Read poems aloud. Argue over them. Complain about prosody. We were there to listen to a recording he had of "The Bonnie Earl of Murray." And sometimes we saw Al's growing collection of signed books by other Canadian

Al Purdy with fellow poet Steven Heighton, 1998

poets. (My favourite dedication among them was "To Awful Al from Perfect Peggy.")

All this changed our lives. It allowed us to take poetry seriously. This happened with and to numerous other young poets all over the country, right until the last days of Al Purdy's life. He wasn't just a "sensitive" man, he was a generous man.

Most of all we should celebrate his fervent, dogmatic desire to write poetry. A glass-blower makes money. A worm-picker has a more steady income. Al, a man who had the looks and manner of a brawler, wanted to be a poet. And what is great is that he was a bad poet for a long time and that didn't stop him. That's where the heroism comes in.

And when he became a good, and then a great poet, he never forgot the significance and importance of those bad poets—they were rather like those small homes and farms north of Belleville, "a little adjacent to where the world is," and about to sink into the earth. He had been there. It gave his work a central core of humbleness, strange word

for Al. It resulted in the double-take in his work, the point where he corrects himself.

"I have been stupid in a poem. . . ."

As he was not ashamed to whisper in a poem— this in a time of mid-century bards. Al never came with bardic trappings.

Who is he like? you ask yourself. And in Canada there is no one.

I can't think of a single parallel in English literature. It almost seems a joke to attempt that. He was this self-taught poet from up the road. What a brave wonder.

So how do we respond to all that Al was and stood for?

When the great Scottish poet Hugh MacDiarmid, who was pretty close to Al in some ways, died, he had become the embodiment of what the country's culture was, and stood for, and stood against. When he died, another Scottish poet, Norman MacCaig said: "Because of his death, this country should observe two minutes of pandemonium."

I have made many new friends since I last wrote you, amongst them Picasso and Braque, who are still working tremendously and very successfully. My new role of "photographer" has made it possible to go everywhere and be much talked of. I say "photographer" because it places me out of the fierce competition amongst the painters here. I have something unique, as Jean Cocteau says "I have delivered painting."

I should like to show in New York this fall, if I can make some arrangement. But it must be well arranged and I must have money. my things are not expensive - they should bring from $25 to $50 a piece. If I can find an efficient friend who will handle the matter, I shall send over a batch of the originals.

The image on the left and the letters above are part of an exhibition of Man Ray's first portfolio of Rayographs (*Les Champs Délicieux*, 1922) on display at the University of Toronto Art Centre during October and November 2000. The two letter fragments are from correspondence between Man Ray and his American patron Ferdinand Howald, from May 1922. The portfolio and letters are from the Ohio State University Library in Columbus, Ohio.

A Spy in the House of Excrement

HELEN GARNER

I RECALL THE PRECISE MOMENT at which I resolved to go to the Spa Resort on Koh Samui, in the Gulf of Thailand, and to subject myself to its famous Cleanse and Fast regime. Someone who'd survived it told me that the Cleansers and Fasters sit about for hours at bare tables, comparing notes in shameless detail on the substances which the gruelling regime caused to issue from their bowels. I was ready to pack my bags, even before she added that one young woman had passed *a small plastic doll*, which her mother told her she'd swallowed in early childhood. This was the detail that decided me to become a spy in the house of excrement.

If you are squeamish, bail out now. Turn to the cookery page. No hard feelings. But before you go, consider this piece of graffiti, written above the toilet in a Paris restaurant:

C'est ici que tombent en ruines
Les grands chefs-d'oeuvre de la cuisine.

IT'S RAINING when my scientific friend J. and I take a clapped-out taxi from Koh Samui airport to the Spa Resort. En route everything looks desperate and squalid. Mangy curs scrounge in roadside bins. Our hearts silently sink. We heave our wheeled suitcases out of the boot, and drag them through puddles and wet sand to Reception. A scattering of vagued-out New Agers are loafing about in an open-sided, cement-floored restaurant. Beyond it a beach, angled palms, a flat sea.

My bungalow with its tiny porch and louvres at first glance seems dark, even primitive. Wonky little fluoro lights are set here and there but only the bedlamp works. In the bathroom, tiles are chipped, window frames softly rotting. The bed, however, with crisp white sheets drawn tight and knotted at the corners, is firm as a board. I drag out my pillow from home and plump it up. Next door J. is washing her hands: the water from her basin pours straight out of an open pipe onto the bare dirt under her window. I lie down feebly under the ceiling fan.

At 4 p.m. all new fasters are invited into a dark library, clogged with large items of furniture and a shelf of execrable paperbacks. By means of a video (and later a more graphic personal demonstration) Buzz, the Australian mentor of the program, tries his best to explain how one self-administers the two daily enemas or "colemas" which are an essential part of the cleanse and fast regime.

Everything he says bewilders and appals me. That huge *bucket*? I have to pump its entire contents into my *colon*? But what is this *colema board* on which you lie in your bathroom? Where do you put your bum? Which way does your head point?

"Be creative!" says Buzz, earnestly friendly with his big bony nose, dazzling eye-whites and toned bare shoulders. "If you want to put your legs up in the air, go for it! You might like to meditate, or call on your guardian angel, if you've got one." If I had one, she would be airlifting me out of here right this minute.

Buzz leads us into a cement enclosure where a Thai woman is preparing the afternoon's colemas for a small, dreamily milling crowd of spaced-out fasters in sarongs. With a composed, mysterious smile she ladles boiling water out of a gas-heated vat into numbered clear plastic buckets, and mixes into it a dark fluid—coffee—then adds a spoon or two of cider vinegar. Yee-ouch. What if I perforate my bowel, poison myself, introduce a bug I'll never get rid of? Ruin completely what remains of my battered old body?

"Let's go out," hisses J., "and buy some Dettol."

We spend the eve of our fast at a table overlooking the smooth water (the rain has stopped) and perusing *Cleanse and Purify Thyself*, a 426-page, often incoherent, and sporadically Christian rave by a certain Dr. Richard Anderson N.D., N.M.D., from whose theories the Spa regime draws its inspiration and its authority. Apparently the traditional North American meat-eater's acidic diet causes the body to secrete a substance called *mucoid plaque*. This lines the intestine, combines with other elements and hardens into toxin-holding layers. For good health one must periodically scour off this plaque.

Dr. Anderson's book features hair-raising photos of the mucoid plaque passed by his acolytes. He himself has spent time hiking in the High Sierras with a friend, eating only salads of the raw herbs they find growing there, and carefully measuring the long strings of mucoid plaque they pass. I keep cracking up as I read, he's so fixated and grandiose, with his claims to be in possession of a revolutionary new truth; but while his theories make me glaze over, I am gripped by the photos, his anecdotes, and letters sent to him by his grateful followers: "I could not believe the filth and slime that came out! And so *much* of it! Where does it all come from? *Amazing*!"

DAY 1: Surprisingly, I sleep deep and still. Early next morning we are given a tiny strip of blotter to lick - a pH test. Mine goes green. This qualifies me to do the fast but no one seems particularly interested. A questionnaire handed out on our arrival is never mentioned again or checked by anyone. (How annoying. I love filling out forms. One of the questions is "When was the last time you had an orgasm?") We are repeatedly told that our health is our own responsibility, that the Spa management "do not profess to be medical authorities or advisors." I note the furrowed brow of a Frenchwoman, who whispers to me that she has done a cleanse several times in her country where, however, things are more . . . supervised.

J. and I have signed on for seven days. The regime goes like this. Five times a day, you gulp down a thick "detox drink" of fruit juice, psyllium and bentonite clay. (All I know about bentonite is that Australian farmers throw it into leaking or algae-infested dams. But I have read T. Coraghessan Boyle's satirical novel *The Road to Wellville*, in which a doctor explains that "psyllium . . . is hydroscopic; . . . it absorbs water and will expand in your stomach, scouring you out as it passes through you just as surely as if a tiny army of janitors were down there equipped with tiny scrub brushes. . . . Like

eating a broom—but that broom will sweep you clean.")

The gluggy doses are staggered with three-hourly handfuls of six capsules: three herbal supplements, and three "chompers" or "intestinal cleansers." Each evening you take a Flora Grow capsule, to replace friendly bacteria in the intestine. You are so sodden with fluids that you are never hungry.

And twice a day you collect your numbered bucket of fluid and retire to your private bathroom. You hang the bucket from a rusty wire hook in the ceiling over the toilet. You take off all your clothes (this can get messy). You lay your four-foot-long colema board down flat, resting the holed end of it over the toilet and balancing the other end on a low plastic stool.

You give a quick suck—as if stealing petrol—to the long plastic tube that drops from the high bucket, and when the fluid starts to flow, you block it off with a large rusty bulldog clip while you get settled on the board. You lie on your back with your knees bent and your bottom over the hole. Your "personal colema tip," like a tiny sprinkler that fits onto the end of the long tube, you anoint with KY jelly; then you slide it a little way into your rectum, lie back on the board, release the bulldog clip, and let warm water from the bucket flow into your lower intestine.

You hold your anal sphincter closed for as long as you can tolerate the steadily growing sensation of fullness, then clamp off the tube and gently massage your abdomen with your fingertips. Then you relax your sphincter. And into the toilet slides a luke-warm gush of . . . we'll get to that in a minute.

Many westerners have bad memories of enemas. As children we were given them for threadworms. Women of my generation going into labour, thirty years ago in a public hospital, were first shaved, then given a rough and hasty enema: an experience sorely humiliating. Yet in alternative healing circles, colonic irrigation has always been popular. Indeed, the practice has a long and chequered history, probably in every culture. Not the least of this is erotic. Upper-class British boys of earlier times, whose colons were briskly washed out by beloved nannies, felt the thrill of it; and Victorian prostitutes would number enemas among their professional services.

Jacqueline Rau, *Alice Gaïffe, Miniaturiste sur ivoire*, 1936

Dr. "Rich" Anderson, whether he's aware of it or not, stands in a long tradition of almost Manichean loathing of the putrefying inner caverns of the human body. His diatribe echoes inarticulately the angst of the great eighteenth century Irish writer and cleric Jonathan Swift: "But Celia, Celia, Celia shits."

Has my learned disquisition got you past the squeamish moment? If not, leave now.

So here I lie, on a chipped white melamine board in the spartan bathroom of the bungalow, letting the water in, letting the water out; and eventually a series of small, soft objects slides out of me into the bowl. I repeat and repeat until the bucket is empty. It takes about 40 minutes. And all the while, a small silvery-brown gecko is perched high on an upright of the window frame, head down, feet spread: I could swear he was watching me.

That evening, after the last drinks and capsules, we're advised to take a bowl of clear vegetable broth. It's the first thing I've put in my mouth all day, apart from the doses and my toothbrush. Just vegetable-flavoured water, really, with a dash of cayenne thrown in; but I approach it avidly, this liquid so clear, so fine, that one can barely believe it would *have* a flavour. It's a large bowl and I eat it slowly, with a dessert spoon, faint with delight at its simplicity and purity.

DAY 2: At 4 a.m. I wake from a dense, dream-filled sleep, imagining bacteria swarming on my "personal colema tip" where it lies on the bathroom shelf. What would my sisters, the nurses, say? "You mean you stick that thing up yourself without sterilising it?" The ceiling fan whirs. Waves on the nearby beach surge and flop. Crickets and frogs keep on seep-seep-seeping in their strange unison. A small motorbike goes screaming past, a hundred metres from my head, along the road to Lamai. What am I doing here? I fantasize scrubbing my colema board with Dettol. Dawn comes and I can't be bothered— so swiftly does one adapt to the unimaginable.

The day crawls along. I do the regime, I sleep, I sprawl in a stupor on a deck chair. I have a massage in the pleasant, open-sided, palm-thatched sala where gentle breezes fan the air. (The Thai masseuses in their loose Spa uniforms wait for requests, sitting in a group near the steam room, murmuring to each other and deftly crocheting toilet roll covers.) Some people are regularly doing yoga, other eager beavers mention a gym. J. is sociable, but I can't bear to hear one more person say "Amaaaaaazing!" I hide in my bungalow and continue to plough through the pile of novels I've brought: *A Change of Climate, The Hours, The Untouchable, Cold Mountain.*

DAY 3: Each day is superficially the same but psychologically distinct. I am weak, vague and hypersensitive. My personal vibe is plummeting. Several young princes of narcissism swan about the place. One in particular grates upon my nerves. He speaks to no one, withholds eye-contact from all but a favoured few, and poses ascetically on the beach and near the restaurant, naked except for a loincloth like a nappy. His body is slim and strong but his face is blank, vain, fanatical; he tosses his clean, thick hair about his shoulders, and adopts flamboyant yoga postures in spots where he is sure to be noticed. If my looks could kill, he'd be stretched out beneath a palm, still beautiful in death.

DAY 4: Escalating misanthropy. J.'s is most exercised by Madame Mysterioso, Psychic and Tarot-Reader. She's a thin, rather dingy-looking, but endearing eternal traveller in a set of bulky hair extensions, a nose-ring and silver bangles, a grubby white crocheted bikini top and a brief sarong. While we peruse her laminated A4 Tarot commercial, she tells us she's "zapping her parasites."

J: What parasites would you have?
MME. M: In India I had a tapeworm [parts her hands in a fisherman's gesture] that long! I was crawling to the cafe! I was eating for two! One meal for the worm and one for me! I was as weak as a kitten!
J: How did you know how long it was?
MME. M: (*airily*) Oh, I passed it.
J: (*grimacing*) How did you get rid of it?
MME. M: (*suavely*) Oh, they have wonderful medicines for worms, in India . . . but I came down here to make sure there was nothing else in there.

She drifts away to the next table. I feel ancient, uncool, too well-scrubbed.

J: I thought I saw disapproval on your face.
H: You're projecting! I thought she was sweet—like Linda Jaivin if she dropped two stone and went feral. Would you get a tarot reading from her?
J: (*promptly*) Nope.
H: Too much bullshit?
J: All I see, when I look at her, is pathology.
H: (*flaring up*) What's pathological about her?
J: (*severely*) She's abandoned her tribe. Her mother wouldn't be able to communicate with her.

There's no point in squabbling: we're both too out of it. I skulk off to lie on my board and brood darkly about what is pathological where families are concerned, and what is simply survival. The little gecko pops out of his hidey-hole and keeps me company, gazing down with his head on one side and his throat pulsing.

Nothing much happens colema-wise till I've almost emptied my bucket—then suddenly a whole lot of slithery stuff comes rushing out. I sit up, disconnect the colema tip, and peer into the toilet: a strange bumpy curved object, like a small brown croissant with a sheen on it. I'm excited. *Can this be the famous mucoid plaque?* I tear the long side off the KY jelly packet and prod the croissant with it. Yes! It's a chunky-nubbly, stringy, almost odourless sort of *chain*. Brilliant!

Dazed with success and starvation, I dismantle the equipment and hose the whole place down. Before I'm done, cramps rack my belly. Soon I'm curled up and groaning on the bed. But I'm not scared. I believe it will pass, and eventually it does.

For the rest of the day I'm in a dream. Speaking is all but impossible. If someone addresses me I take ages to focus on their face, process what they've said, and dredge up a suitable reply. "I feel we're losing you," says motherly, scientific J. "You seem other-worldly, as if you've left your body." With shy pride I describe my mucoid plaque. "Huh," she says. "It's probably only psyllium plus gel from the capsules." "What?" I cry, aghast, "you mean it's all just *hype*?" She shrugs and turns away.

DAY 5: My revulsion from the detox drinks and capsules intensifies by the hour. Gagging, I venture into the steam room, grope to the tiled bench, and sit meekly in my sarong, hands clasped on knees. The air is white with fog. Am I even alone? A tall dark mass enters. I squeak, "Who's there?" It's a man from San Diego, who tells me the tale of his gallstones. As it happens I have already heard it around the traps, for he is the legend of our intake: people point to him and whisper, "See that guy? He's been fasting for, like, ever."

"We all have gallstones," he says, in the nonchalant but slightly faint voice characteristic of someone more than seven days into the program. "I did the epsom salt treatment. I passed a thousand stones at first, then two and maybe even three thousand more. I lost a lot of them through the weave of the plastic sieve."

Gallstones? Do gallstones come out your bum? My croissant suddenly doesn't seem worth mentioning. I sit in silence, outclassed, adrift in a world obsessed with filth. Everybody seems so *sure*. The printed instructions for the fast warn us against "negative people" who may bring us down at vulnerable moments. Fancying myself an intellectual as I do, I consider it a matter of honour, in this credulous environment, to be one of those "negative people"—but what *do* I actually know about the inner workings of the body? What is the basis for my scepticism? I'm still functioning on Miss Featherstone's biology lessons at school, her simple diagram of a mouse: cheese went in at the top, moved down the tubes, and issued from the bottom in what she called "little—black—pellets."

A night of despair. At 3 a.m., the death hour, a hoarse, hiccuping, humanoid cry—"HUCK-haaaah!"—erupts from inside the wall right by my head. Heart athump, I kick the wall, then sit up in the dark and curse. I can't go on with this. It's masochistic—it's insane. How can I get out of here? At dawn I meet J. in the sandy courtyard. She says, "I'm absolutely desolate. I hardly slept. In the night I thought, 'I could just stand up and put my head among those fan blades'." We exchange haggard looks. I whisper, "Wanna throw in the towel?" A pause. She sets her jaw. "No."

We trudge to the detox counter. "Gee, I feel cranky," I mutter to Henri (pron. AhnREE), a cheery sixty-plus American know-it-all, with grey curly hair and faded tatts, who has famously been on the road for the last seventeen years, carrying only a light rucksack, and managing his investments from internet cafes. "Ah," he says wisely, "if you'd done a cleanse as many times as I have, you'd know to expect this. It's just the toxins coming out."

Toxins, shmoxins. What is a bloody toxin, anyhow? I stump away to the restaurant and sneak a big carrot juice. Jackie, an investment banker from London, tells me the horrid HUCK-haaaah creature of the night is "probably some sort of lizard." Yeah, right.

AhnREE joins the table of fasters. In three minutes flat he has skilfully derailed our bowel-centred conversation and is presenting his credentials as a sage. These stem from his glory days as a hippy, which must be as remote to his audience of young American guys as is the Civil War: "Back in the sixties, my former wife and I, we bought a Winnebago! We drove right across the United States—visiting communes!" When he leaves the table for his massage I expect us all to dive back into coarse boasting about our heroic feats of self-purification; but a deferential silence falls, then one of the Americans—the one I have until this moment liked best, a cute version of George in *Seinfeld*—sighs and says, "AhnREE's great. I really respect his *nomadship*."

J. reports having seen Madame Mysterioso out in the courtyard the night before, "doing a sort of dance. With bells on her feet. If I'd had a gun I would have blown her away. She's to me what the narcissist in the loin-cloth is to you." Grimly we fantasize a sten gun swivel-mounted on the verandah rail, and begin *sotto voce* to draw up a list. Sorry, AhnREE, but you're on it.

After what would have been lunch, J. and I nick across the road and through a coconut grove to a flasher, newer resort. Oh, an oasis of luxury. It has *lawns*. It has *glass tables*. It has alternating *blue and green tiles*. But even as we relax, guiltily, in the perfumed elegance of its sofa cushions, we experience a pang of loyalty to our battling old outfit down below, with its chipped bathrooms, its hard-labouring Thais who could only afford these treatments by winning the lottery; its spacey rationale, its credulous spirituality, its bizarre theories—and its dim little cabins full of westerners pumping filtered water into their bowels and then studying, theorising about, marvelling at and saying a jubilant farewell to the muck that comes out. We slip our thongs on and scurry home.

心の旅路

夫婦愛の眞情……
感激の名篇愈々登場!

グリア・ガースン 主演
ロナルド・コールマン

マーヴィン・ルロイ 監督
M.G.M映画

Random Harvest

DAY 6: How slowly, slowly, in a blur of detox, capsules and colemas, each day passes! The thick drinks and distasteful capsules I force down with a shudder, but I must admit that I like the colemas. Quite a lot, actually. J. entertains herself during hers by listening to talking books on a Walkman, but I love just lying there in the cool, staring up at the criss-cross weave of the ceiling and listening to sounds drifting in from the world: cars and scooters on the road, someone scrubbing, water trickling, a breeze rattling in palm fronds, a Thai voice raised in sharp chatter. Birds chirp in their business-like way.

This dreamy pleasure can only be infantile—the body's memory of lying swaddled in the cot, long, long before toilet-training, and being languorously aware of one's bowels. Sensing their fullness without guilt or anxiety, and being allowed to let go.

After each colema I take a shower, curl up on my bed for a while, then dress and stroll out to the beach. It's a plain, beautiful curve, shaded by palms and visited by high-prowed fishing boats. A steady, pleasant breeze blows across it, always from the same direction. In the distance comes and goes a line of mountains, faint as a mirage.

And yet the regime is a strain, an assault. Nothing here is imposed; there is no big stick; one has to find the discipline within oneself. Fasters greet each other with nods, and sit in a stunned row on palm-shaded deckchairs outside the restaurant. The non-fasting Spa guests, of whom there are plenty, look up from their plates of exquisite tropical food and stare at us with awe—or is it merely pity? My emotional state lurches between rapture and dejection. Fresh revelations of the obvious ("Time passes! Youth does not last! Life is short!") strike me the crushing blows familiar from long-ago acid trips. Somehow, though, one emerges from sloughs of despond, and slogs on.

There are three sets of scales at the Spa, though even the management jokes about their unreliability. A charming young Bostonian couple on their honeymoon, who have been fasting and cleansing for ten days, are collectively two stone lighter. J. is crestfallen that she has lost only one kilo. She gets on her mobile to a Sydney gym bunny, who reassures her: "It's all fluid, darling! It'll drop off when you come home!" I, catastrophically, seem to have lost weight only from where I most need to keep it: my face.

But you can see a change in people's eyes and skin: clarity, freshness, brightness. To look at the face of the Gallstone Legend from San Diego, on day thirteen of the cleanse and still counting, is to contemplate the pure, sensitive lineaments of boyhood.

DAY 7: Today we are to break our fast. We are advised to eat, that first incredulous afternoon, "only" a plate of sliced papaya. How gluttonous it seems, to approach that pile of glistening orangey-pink slivers! When the moment comes, we pick up our spoons with a strange dreaminess, reluctant to break the spell. And yes, it does taste good, and feels even better—but there's a kind of disappointment in it, too. Now everything will become ordinary again. The days will be divided by those weird social events called meals. We could have salads this evening, or soups. But, still in love with our self-discipline, we pick at the delicious food without appetite.

I play Scrabble by candle-light with a new arrival, a green-eyed boy from Long Island. He is ambitious and beats me hands down. In my vagueness I let the candle burn to a stump and set fire to the edge of his plastic board. He cannot conceal his annoyance, but this new, purified me smiles at him, maddeningly no doubt, out of the deep well of my tranquillity. Secretly I long to have become a fanatic like San Diego Man and fasted for, like, *ever*.

DAY 8: Departure time approaches and we all become light-headed, hilarious. I find myself fooling and laughing with people I've wanted to gun down, in the throes of our ordeal (though nothing can redeem Narcissus in his nappy). Jackie, the curly-headed London banker whose sly wit has re-prieved several nincompoops from our firing squad, remarks happily, "I feel as if my personality's come back, since I started eating again."

That's it exactly, and it's happening all around us. Am I just light-headed, or has the moustachio'd bore metamorphosed into a wit, the *M*A*S*H* addict revealed a passion for Henry James, the prune-lipped divorcee begun to weep for joy in a deck chair, the neurotic Jewish mother at last turned off her mobile? Nothing but euphoria, wherever I turn.

Late that day I sit under a palm tree and watch Madame Mysterioso, her fake plaits flopping on her shoulders, emerge shining from a swim in the sea and walk slowly back to her towel. She lies on her back, rests a moment, then raises both knees and rolls her back right over like a hedgehog's, till her knees are touching the sand behind her shoulders. The knobs of her curved spine gleam in the low sun. She is so slender, so relaxed, her muscles so delicately and firmly defined, her posture so beautiful, that I find myself contemplating her, for the first time, with something like respect.

Book Tour Comix # 911 ...
The Television Interview

MARGARET ATWOOD

Shrimp Étouffée

HAROLD WEBER

A J. LIEBLING'S account of Louisiana politics, The Earl of Louisiana, opens with the observation that "Southern political personalities, like sweet corn, travel badly. They lose flavour with every hundred yards away from the patch." Most writers attempting to understand the byzantine nature of Louisiana's political life would probably have made the more conventional connection between politics, sex, and money, a trinity on display, for instance, in the trial of Edwin Edwards, prodigious womaniser and gambler as well as three-time governor of that august state. Liebling, however, unerringly captures the essence of Louisiana in the simile that unites food and politics, the belly and not the groin or pocketbook the central term of its existence.

I was lucky enough to live in Louisiana for seven years and the following recipe always reminds me of the decadence, political and otherwise, that I relished during my years there. Shrimp étouffée ("smothered" or "suffocated") is a traditional Cajun dish, this version cobbled together from half-a-dozen Louisiana junior-league cookbooks with a friend (Jerry Speir) whose Louisiana birth gives this recipe whatever authenticity it possesses. I enjoy making this dish not only for its taste, but because of the preparation of the roux, one of the few cooking tasks worth the bother of stirring for thirty to forty minutes without interruption. Even after dozens of repetitions of this recipe I still take pleasure in the care necessary to combine flour and butter properly; the process, as well as the result, is voluptuous.

INGREDIENTS

½ pound (2 sticks) unsalted butter
1 cup flour
2 green peppers, chopped
2 medium onions, chopped
1½ bunches green onions, chopped
3 cups chopped celery
water
1½ to 2 pounds shrimp, shelled
salt
pepper
cayenne
Worcestershire sauce
Tabasco sauce
chopped parsley

Making the roux: After melting the butter over a medium-low flame in a large, heavy pot or kettle—cast-iron providing the greatest authenticity—slowly add the flour a little at a time, carefully stirring to incorporate each addition fully. After you've added all the flour, continue to stir as the mixture simmers. During this time the roux is both volatile and dangerous: it will quickly burn itself if unattended, and you if splattered. Gradually the dense mixture of flour and butter will get thinner and begin to change colour. After twenty minutes I become anxious, but eventually the roux will transform itself, become darker and darker, and finally achieve a rich reddish-brown. You can now proceed to make the étouffée, though the flour in the roux remains so over powering that it hardly pays to taste the dish for the first two hours. Only gradually does the roux begin to develop its nutty flavour, aided by a brave and heavy hand with the spices. Be vulgar: Cajun cuisine is earthy, not sophisticated, and Louisianians consider this a spicy dish.

After the roux has turned colour, add half of the chopped vegetables—again, keep your face out of the pot: the roux splatters easily at this point—stir vigorously for a minute or two to coat them thoroughly with the roux, and then add enough water, which you've brought almost to the boil on another burner, to make the gravy. A proper cookbook might describe the gravy as thick enough to coat a spoon; ideally it should be almost, but not quite, impossible to place anything beside the étouffée on a plate, since the gravy should run enough so that it isn't quite absorbed by the rice that the étouffée is served on, but requires the final sop of a crusty French bread.

Partially cover the pot and simmer over a low flame, stirring occasionally, for three to four hours. During this time a crust will periodically form on top of the étouffée: mix it in whenever you stir. You will also have to add hot water occasionally as the étouffée gets too thick. While the mixture simmers you can continue to taste and add spices. About an hour before serving, add the rest of the chopped vegetables and remove the cover entirely. About fifteen minutes before serving, add the shelled shrimp and a handful of minced parsley.

Serve over rice with a loaf of French bread. For those who must, brown rice will do, though such gestures to health and nutrition betray the dish's heritage. This is emphatically not good for you. I recommend a white basmati rice, whose nutty flavour compliments the étouffée. Serves six comfortably.

Jacqueline Rau,
*Gérard Mulys,
chorégraphe*, 1937

Simonides and the Art of Negative Attention

ANNE CARSON

SIMONIDES OF KEOS was the smartest man in the fifth century B.C., or so I have come to suspect. There are many ways in which I could exemplify this. For example, negatively. Any reader of Simonidean verse in its original Greek is immediately struck by a singular fact. The poet's syntax is overwhelmingly negative. Let me be more specific. Simonides negates a sentence six times as often as his most celebrated contemporary, the poet Pindar. This fact is not incidental nor merely linguistic. Simonides' play with negative syntax gives a good introduction to the originality of his mind and technique. Within the process of negation Simonides confronts questions that were to exercise artistic practice and intellectualist speculation for the rest of the fifth century B.C. He also confronts himself. Negation is a shape that characterizes not only the poet's syntax but also his concepts, epistemology, and biographical persona.

Not for no reason, I begin with an anecdote. One day Simonides and William Safire were sitting in a bar chatting about language, when Simonides turned to his companion and said, "Isn't it a curious thing that both of us have in our respective languages a phenomenon whereby two negative words or expressions combine to form one positive meaning, the so-called 'double negative,' but the converse phenomenon, whereby two positive words add up to a single negative meaning, does not occur?" Safire glanced up wearily from his drink and said, "Yeah, yeah."

The anecdote is a useful one for illustrating how powerful an effect can be obtained by a speaker who causes an affirmative statement to transform itself into a negative one. When "yes" turns into "no" there is a sudden vanishing and a shift to new meaning, there is a tilt and realignment of the listener's world-view. Simonides is a master of such transformations. He says "no" more often than any other poet of his period. If we compare the extant corpus of his poetry, which contains roughly 1300 legible words, with comparable samples of verse from the contemporary poets Anakreon, Pindar, and Bacchylides, the following statistic emerges: in 1300 words of Anakreon we find the negative adverbs ou and me employed 28 times; 1300 words of Pindar render 16 usages of ou and me; 1300 words of Bacchylides give us 19 instances of ou and me. The count for Simonides is 56.

The high ratio of Simonidean negativity depends, in no small degree, on his inclination to form even positive statements negatively, that is, his fondness for the double negative. So, for example, when Simonides wishes to assert that human life contains suffering, he says, "Nothing is not painful among men" or "Not even the men of old who were sons of gods had lives that were not filled with pain and death and danger." Instead of saying "Pleasure is good," he says, "Without pleasure not even a god's life is enviable." Rather than "Virtue is difficult," he says, "No one attains virtue into whom heartbiting sweat does not come." To describe a weeping woman he has the phrase "with cheeks not unwet by tears." To describe a sound which spreads far and wide, he says, "No leaf-shaking blast of wind arose which would have prevented the sound from spreading far and wide." In order to celebrate the fact that the city of Tegea has survived a war, Simonides says, "The smoke of Tegea burning did not rise up into the clear air." And in the famous poem known from Plato's *Protagoras*, Simonides addresses himself to the definition of virtue by setting out twelve negative and double-negative formulations in the space of forty lines of verse, leading to the resoundingly Spinozan conclusion, "All things to be sure are beautiful into which ugly things are not mixed."

It would be an insult to the care which this poet lavishes upon telling us what is not the case to dismiss his negativity as accidental, incidental, or rhetorical. His poetic action insistently, spaciously, and self-consciously posits in order to deny. (The poet's awareness of his own taste and tactic flashes out, for example, in "Not from fragrant painted flowers . . . but from the bitter thyme I suck my verse.") To read him is a repeated experience of loss, absence, or deprivation from the reader who watches one statement or substantive after another snatched away by a negative adverb, pronoun, or subordinate clause. Simonides' poetic imagination conjures so vividly events that did not occur, people who were not present, possibilities which cannot be expected, that these come to rival the reality which is present and actual. No other poet of the period manages to deny so much, so well. What is Simonides up to?

A prior question cannot be avoided. What is a negative?

A negative is a verbal event. There are, philosophers assure us, no negatives in nature, where every situation is positively what it is. The negative is a peculiarly linguistic resource whose power resides with the user of words. But verbalization in itself is not sufficient to generate the negative. Negation depends upon an act of the imagining mind. In order to say "the smoke of Tegea burning did not rise up into the clear air," I bring together in my mind two pieces of data, one of which is present and actual (Tegea itself perceptible before me), the other of which is absent and fictitious (Tegea as it would be if it were burning). I put these two data together and say, "this is not that." Negation requires this collusion of the present and the absent on the screen of imagination. The one is measured against the other and found to be discrepant; the discrepant datum is annihilated by a word meaning "no." The interesting thing about a negative, then, is that it posits a fuller picture of reality than does a positive statement. And the person who speaks negatively can be said to command and display a more complete view of things than one who makes positive assertions.

Now the ancient poet is by definition someone who commands a fuller view of reality than other people. According to a venerable Greek tradition the poet is sophos ("wise") and his activity is sophia ("wisdom"): to see and to teach a vision of life from which the particularity of our ordinary experience ordinarily excludes us. But Simonides lived on the brink of a time when new and severe pressures would be placed on poetry to justify its claim to special wisdom. Simonides was a forerunner of what is called the Greek "enlightenment," that intense period of fifth-century intellectualism when the sophists launched their critique of poetic wisdom and set about devising a science of dialectic to replace poetic teaching. Simonidean negativity represents a certain prescience on Simonides' part toward the new age of marketable enlightenment. Simonides anticipated the sophistic critique and co-opted its science.

IT WAS ESSENTIALLY a science of measurement, famously summarized by Protagoras in the words "Man is the measure of all things—both of the things that are, that they are, and of the things that are not, that they are not." Other fifth-century intellectuals would interest themselves in measuring geometrical angles, intervals of music, spaces between stars. Simonides predicted them all by locating his measuring inside poetic method. And whereas Protagoras prided himself on a technical ability to argue both sides of any case and published two textbooks of Antilogika ("Contrary Arguments"), Simonides for his part constructed poems in the shape of antilogika, painting a picture of things that moves inclusively over the negative and the positive, defining the things that are by excluding the things that are not, evoking the absent in order to measure it against the present. The technique would impress any sophist but the poet's aim is not technical, nor is his measuring sophistic. It is a mode of knowledge, perhaps best described in terms borrowed from philosophy. It was the fifth-century philosopher Parmenides who

said to the seeker after truth, "You must gaze steadily at what is absent as if it were present by means of your mind." It was the twentieth-century philosopher Bergson who characterized philosophic speculation as "making use of the void to think the full." When Simonides pictures the world in relations of denial and absence, he is using the power of the negative reality free from sophistic subjectivism. For Protagoras, man is the criterion of what exists; his logos makes nothing of reality. The Simonidean logos says "no" to that nothing. For an example of the converse phenomenon we might look to the usage of another sophist cleric of a more recent and arguably less robust Enlightenment, George Eliot's Casaubon: "'Yes,' said Mr. Casaubon, with that peculiar pitch

of voice which makes the word half a negative."

Perhaps the most poignant example of Simonides making use of the void in order to think the full is his tiny poem on time:

> *Being man, you can't ever say what will happen tomorrow*
> *nor, seeing a prosperous fellow, how long will it last.*
> *For swift—not even of a longwinged fly*
> *so! the change.*

It is a poem so tiny it manages to vanish as you read it, not only into the past but into non-existence. At the end you find yourself staring at an event that did not take place. The first three verses prepare this vanishing point by means of a series of contractions. As you proceed from verse one through verse four, each line is shorter than the one before it. The units of syntax progressively simplify. The metrical units are reduced, from choriambic metra with dactylic expansion in verse one, to choriambic metra alone in verse two, to dactyls in verse three, and finally, in verse four, to an indefinable metrical shape not quite a choriamb not quite a dactyl. The units of thought dramatically diminish, from the universal "man" of verse one, to an individual "prosperous fellow" in verse two, who dwindles to a fly in verse three, which vanishes in verse four. And time itself shrinks sharply, from the foreverness of "ever . . . tomorrow" in verse one, to a specific measurement of "how long" in verse two, which contracts a mere attribute of swiftness in verse three, and even that vanishes in verse four into "change." Change is where you end up, but, by the time you get there, the change to which the word refers is not only retrospective, it is retrospectively negated. As you glance back from "change" to the negative adverb "not even" looming above it, you realize that the fly in this poem has not only shifted its wings, it has flown right out of the argument, relegated to the category of a negative exemplum. Like time itself, the fly is present only as an absence.

The poet's control of time is a power vested in negativity. Once we have invented time, and we have, we can only escape it by refusing to know what time it is. Consider, for example, an early painting of Cezanne called *The Black Clock*. It is a painting of a clock with a face but no hands, that is, a picture of timelessness. A clock without hands designates no particular time and all possible times at the same time. A clock without hands is a powerful image of the vantage-point taken by the poet as his *logos* ranges forward and backward in time and the rest of us stand, lodged in our partial view of reality, eyes fixed on the moment we call "the present." Meanwhile we should not overlook the fact that the clock face on which Cezanne captures timelessness is a black one: an act of painterly negation. We might also recall the opening shot of the movie *Floating Weeds*, a 1933 masterpiece of the Japanese filmmaker Ozu. This film concerns the effects of passing time on a travelling company of Kabuki players and begins in the waiting room of a railway station: the camera is positioned so that it looks out from inside the glass cabinet of an enormous stopped grandfather clock.

TO REFUSE TO KNOW what time it is, is an almost godlike gesture. The mind that can deny time can say "no" to mortality, as Simonides did repeatedly and famously throughout his career, for he was the most prolific composer of epitaphs in the Greek tradition and widely celebrated for his funeral songs. It is a nice puzzle whether the outstanding negativity of this poet is cause or effect of the fact that he spent so much of his time in the company of the Great Gainsayer. Certainly death gives most of us our elemental experience of absent presence, and an epitaph might be thought of as a vanishing point—or a sort of concrete double negative—where the absence of life disappears into the presence of death and nullifies itself. Certainly the poet's power to negate the negating action of death derives from his special view of reality, a view which sees death everywhere and finds life within it, a view which perceives presence as absence and finds a way to turn that relation inside out. Certainly this paradox of absent presence, forming itself as an act of negation, is the shape built into Simonides' concepts and syntax and poetic technique, and also into many of the stories he tells in his verse. But we should not fail to notice that it is also a shape recurrent in the stories told about Simonides, that is, the mass of anecdotes transmitted to us from antiquity as his biographical persona. Consider the following stories from the traditional vita of Simonides.

ONCE SIMONIDES was feasting at the table of the tyrant Hieron in Syracuse and noticed that roast hare was being served to all the other guests, but not to him; the absent presence of roast hare moved Simonides to compose a small epigram. Once Simonides was dining with friends on a hot day and saw that the waiters were mixing snow into everyone else's wine, but not into his, whereupon he was inspired to compose a small epigram. Once Simonides was commissioned to write a poem in honour of the Thessalian prince Skopas. When he performed the poem Skopas was displeased, charging that the poet had allotted too many verses to the gods and too few to Skopas. The prince therefore denied Simonides one half of his poetic fee, instructing him to seek the rest from the gods. This incident provoked Simonides to create not another poem but his famous memory system. Another

anecdote tells us that Simonides kept in his house two boxes in which to store the charis ("grace" or "recompense") received for his poems: one box for money, one box for gratitude. The second box was always empty. Finally, Simonides is alleged by the Suda to have added four letters to the Greek alphabet (eta, omega, psi, and chi). Alongside these anecdotes we should note an enigmatic sentence from the Simonidean testimonia:

> . . . Simonides advises us to play at life and to be 100% serious about nothing . . . .

To be 100% serious about nothing, about absence, about the void which is fullness, is the destiny and task of the poet. These biographical vignettes are not stories of Simonidean greed, as they are conventionally interpreted. Rather, they offer a paradigm of the poetic consciousness in its relation to everyday reality. The poet is someone who feasts at the same table as other people. But at a certain point he feels a lack. He is provoked by a perception of absence within what others regard as a full and satisfactory present. His response to this discrepancy is an act of poetic creation; he proceeds by means of his poetic sophia to make present in the mind what is lacking from the actual. One more story from the Simonidean vita will help us focus this paradigm. It is a story of annihilation and miraculous escape, a story about making use of the void to think the full, a story in which the poet gazes steadily at what is absent and makes it become present by means of his mind— the story of how Simonides came to invent his memory system.

Once Simonides was dining in the house of Skopas of Thessaly with a number of other guests when a servant appeared at his elbow to say that two young men were asking for him at the front door. Simonides left the table and hurried to the door but found no one there. Meanwhile, behind him, the roof of the house collapsed, crushing Skopas and all the other banqueters. This calamity at first appeared to have cancelled not only the lives but also the afterlives of Skopas and his guests, for the bodies were too mangled to permit identification for burial. But Simonides saved the day. He returned to the dining room and was able to conjure up mentally the exact location of every guest at the table. He filled in the absent presences and attached to each a name and a memory. By means of his poetic technology, Simonides doubled the negative of death and said "no" to oblivion.

IT IS A NOT UNINTERESTING coincidence, whose decoding I leave with you, that the stories of which Simonides is the author and the stories in which Simonides figures as protagonist betray a rich and strange similarity. An unforgettable shape of absence is in them. As historians we are wary of such coincidences, alert to a tendency within literary biography to read the nature of a poet's poetry back into his life as personal event. So, for example, Anakreon was said to have perished by choking on a grape seed, while Sappho jumped off a cliff for love of a young man, and Tolstoy died waiting for a train. But it is a very rich reading that can bring down the roof of a house and crush a roomful of banqueters.

On the other hand, Simonides was a very greedy poet. And surely a poet must be greedy for reality if he is to transcribe his perception of the whole of things. Why did Simonides bother to invent four new letters for the Greek alphabet? Presumably, from a certain sense of cognitive pique. He heard these sounds being pronounced in people's speech, he saw no symbol for them in the written language, he refused to tolerate this partial transcription of reality. He sat down and filled in the absent presences, by means of his mind. It is a mind that sees its own task clearly: to pay attention to absence wherever absence occurs. It is a task that sets Simonides against sophistic subjectivism, against the limitations of mortality, against time itself—for the task is endless. Nothing fails to escape Simonides, forever.

Waving Out of the Train Window

for Victor Anant 1928–1999

JOHN BERGER

I AM LOOKING at a painting by the Indian artist Bhupen Khakhar. He painted it two years ago. It shows the man-god Sri Rama, who has a loincloth of flames, embracing the monkey-god Hanuman, the monkey's face pressed against the man's shoulder. Impossible to tell whether it represents a moment of greeting or farewell. I have thought of it often recently.

FOLLOWING THE DIAMOND of his quick intelligence, the cards detach themselves lightly from his hand and are placed on the table with a minimum of movement or gesture. I think he does this to underline the silence of the game. He enjoys this silence.

In a southern suburb of Paris, where he stayed from time to time, Victor Anant discovered a bridge club. He scarcely spoke a word of French, yet the members lined up to be his partner because he could hide his cunning with something of the same elegance as nature does, and to share in this was a rare pleasure. It was in Bombay that he first learnt to play bridge, in Bombay where he worked as a sports journalist and was a militant in the Congress Socialist Party, led by Gandhi, struggling for Indian independence. In his last novel, *Sacred Crow*, he wrote about his own grandmother.

He looked at his grandmother. Even with the generations between them, the resemblance was unmistakable. Same slightly domed forehead; clean-cut ears; long neck; shoulders sloping; arched feet; smoother brown skin; and the same small hips and rounded buttocks.

"It won't be long before lunch is ready," she said and went on cleaning the rice.

"Here, let me do that, save your eyes."

Sparks of mischief looked at him through wrinkled eyes. "I can still pick out the tiniest stones, and anyway it's nearly done." Her finger moved fast.

"Kunjamma, I came to ask you something about our family."

"What is it?"

"Is there a streak of madness in us?" He was surprised he put it so bluntly.

She played with her beads. She thought for a while. "Madness, no. Ahankaaram, egotism, pride, obstinacy, terrible rage, recklessness, yes. Madness, no."

"Then why did Grandfather die as he did?"

"Oh him," she chuckled. Played with her beads again.

"Tell me, it troubles me."

"Blazing fires die like that."

"Was he a good man?"

"He was upright. . . ."

When he came home from the bridge club, he would refer to one or two of the more dramatic games. He repeated the bids he had made in a light sing-song voice as if they were incantations. "Five Clubs called and made!" "Four No Trumps with only two aces and we got them!"

We were friends for forty-five years. We first met in the Parcel Office of Paddington Station. He was working there, and I tracked him down out of curiosity, for I had read a sparkling article about the Christmas season in London, which he had just written and published. A few months before, he had arrived from Bombay. He was wearing a railwayman's cap. He lived in a bedsitting room on the ground floor of a boarding house in Sussex Gardens, two minutes away from the station.

I'm now in a French train going to Toulouse.

How many times did you and I meet and say goodbye in railway stations? On a Paddington platform I remember handing over to you a haversack of raw beet roots which I'd brought from Gloucester.

On a Victoria platform you ask me whether I've forgotten my sandwiches. Egg sandwiches. Daphne made them, you say.

Waving out of the train door windows. Scribbling in notebooks at airports, waiting for a plane arriving late from Delhi, Dar es Salaam, Kampala, New York. . . .

On a platform at King's Cross with the train pulling out for Scotland—take the mandarins, you bloody fool, take them.

Leaving was not heavy for there were the egg sandwiches, the dried bananas to unwrap, and the latest book to read and later argue about. It seems to me that, forty years ago, we argued for six whole months about Saul Bellow's novel *The Adventures of Augie March*.

Your journeys were often much longer than mine. There was always, however, the tacit understanding between us that we'd be able to scrape up enough money for a return ticket, should the need arise. I remember wiring you money in Djibouti for the return ticket!

This, Donkey, is what makes me smile now in the train going to Toulouse.

I don't remember when he first started calling me Monkey. Out of revenge and rhyme, I called him Donkey.

How are the nuts, Monkey?

You can't ask that any more, I tell him, you're dead.

I WATCH the french trees, fields, roads slipping past the train window, and I suspect I don't see you because I'm not concentrating hard enough. Maybe I should meditate.

Monkey, forget it, you say. Just go down to Betanzos, buy the bread at the corner bakers where they know you, put it under your shirt so it stays warm from the oven, and drive on your bike back to the house, where Nella and I are waiting with coffee for breakfast, as fast as you can! That's as far as you can get, you, with meditation!

You died at 6 a.m. this morning, the 19th of October 1999.

In Wandsworth, North London, if you want to be precise, you add.

I think you died like you made rice, not letting it cook a moment too long, touching it with one finger, remembering a gesture of your grand-

Victor Anant

mother's, and then taking it off the fire.

I'll go to Betanzos and find you among the white buildings.

The drawing of the white building you gave me is in Karachi now.

This morning in this fucking French train you are between me and everything I can see, making no difference at all. Almost no difference. A few things have gotten a little sharper.

Gotten! Why do you suddenly use an Americanism? Are you hoping to sell this shit in the

States? If so you can give me straightaway fifty per cent! If I hadn't died, what would you have to write about? Nothing.

Everything, Donkey, everything. I use the American gotten because it makes the word a bit sharper, according to my ear. And since 6 a.m. this morning, even round things, like a ring, have gotten sharper, distinctly sharper.

> Under the paperweight of grief
> the silk paper of
> your incontestable touch
> which never the less
> nevertheless
> will be blown away
> and later return
> to assuage
> only God knows today
> what pain to come,
> Donkey.

IN THE OLD CENTRE of Toulouse is the basilica of St. Sernin. Nine centuries old and very tall. I walk in and look up, the same as everyone else does. It was built to make people look up. And, way above, the arches lay their hands on the heads of those looking up. So far and no further, their gesture says. This is Romanesque, no excess here. The arches lay their hands on your bald head and on your domed forehead which is like your grandmother's. The columns and arches are the colour of sticks of celery and your bald head is the colour of a candle flame reflected in copper.

I buy a candle for you. (Five francs.)

It's tall, about a fifth of the length of a billiard cue. What was the name of the pub in Belsize Park where we used to play snooker? At lunch time, because at night, in those days, you were sub-editing on the *Guardian*. This was before you had your jazz column in the *Guardian*. Remember when we drove all night through northern France listening to the jazz you'd write about the following week? In the Belsize Park pub, you had a steadier hand than me, a better eye, a more accurate memory, and a prestigious sense of punctuation, the last coming, I suspect, from your railwayman father and his punctuality, which for him, quite apart from the trains, was also a holy attribute.

Maybe there is something in common, I wonder, between certain Brahmans and certain Benedictine monks, in both cases their faith makes them punctual?

Crap Monkey!

Being so tall, the candle will burn quite a long while, Donkey.

I light it from one of the other candles already burning. As the wick catches I remember your saying how you'd like to be buried beside a very small Romanesque chapel—no bigger than a Paddington bedsitting room—at the top of a hill in La Paz, near Betanzos, Galicia.

How many times did we walk up there through the eucalyptus forest to lean our backs against its brick wall at the end of the day? The bricks were the same colour as those used here in Toulouse for the tower of the basilica. Same colour, baked in the same century. Through our shirts we felt the warmth of the sun stored in the chapel walls all summer long.

I could be put in one of these drawers, you said one evening, whilst nodding at the tombs, let into the cemetery wall below the chapel, do you think they'd have me? They'll have you, I replied. I didn't know then that you were going to be hustled out of La Paz.

After one of our visits to the chapel, squatting on the porch of your house, we put on a cassette of Faiz reading his poetry, and whilst I blew on the fire to make it hot enough for the fish you were going to cook, you translated the poems for us.

O Evening be kind,
evening in the city of friends,
be gentle with us. . . .

Towering above the porch of that house are two oak trees which you brought into the stories you wrote by listening to the sound of their leaves. My ears, you said pulling at their lobes, are getting as big as an elephant's. Then, pulling up your *dhoti*, you squatted with your usual ease, to cook the fish.

Today it's hard for me to distinguish in my memory the rustle of the oak leaves and your voice translating Faiz.

Now I have the candle in my hand and I hesitate where to place it. I was thinking of placing it in the back row, beside the dozen other candles burning to accompany prayers already said this morning for the living or the dead. On an impulse I don't. Instead I place it alone in the row nearest to me, where as yet there are no other candles.

After an instant I understand why. Of all the dead, you, I think, are going to remain the nearest to me. Not because you died yesterday. Not because I love you more than anybody—though love you I do. Not for any comparative reason.

It was part of our small conspiracy. Death always came with us, not as a subject of conversation, not as a cautionary reminder, but as a referee to whom we could refer with raised eyebrows. When we were in doubt about the rules—and this happened very often—we would silently refer to him, and listen to his verdict, and nod at the same time, with, strangely, the same expression.

Early yesterday morning the referee counted you out, yet he won't take you far away for we were a trio, and he was used to our company. This is why you'll remain the nearest of the dead for me and why one day you'll tell me what to do.

A Conversation with Edwidge Danticat

ELEANOR WACHTEL

*E*DWIDGE DANTICAT *was born in Port au Prince, the capital of Haiti, the poorest country in the Americas, with the highest infant mortality rate, the lowest life expectancy, and about fifty per cent literacy. When Edwidge was two years old, her father left for New York City. Her mother joined him two years later, leaving Edwidge and a younger brother with an uncle, a minister, and his wife and grandson.*

When Edwidge was twelve, she joined her parents (and two new younger brothers) in Brooklyn. Fluent in French and Creole, she had to learn English and endure epithets from classmates who labelled her a "boat person." "My primary feeling the whole first year was one of loss," she has said. "Loss of my childhood, and of the people I'd left behind—and also of being lost. It was like being a baby—learning everything for the first time."

She recovered the past—her own life and her country's—through her fiction. And at an astonishingly young age, Edwidge Danticat has become one of America's most celebrated novelists. Six years ago, when she was scarcely twenty-five years old, she published her first novel, Breath, Eyes, Memory *which evokes elements of her childhood and traumatic uprooting. It was chosen for Oprah's Book Club and sold more than 600,000 copies. Danticat's next book,* Krik! Krak! *was about story-telling, life under dictatorship, escape to the United States. It was nominated for a National Book Award. Two years ago, still not quite thirty years old, she published her second novel, an ambitious book called* The Farming of Bones. *Here she goes back to a pivotal moment in Hait-*

ian history: the 1937 massacre of more than 15,000 Haitians who were working in the neighbouring Dominican Republic. The story is told by a young Haitian servant, Amabelle, whose parents drown while fleeing for their lives.

This interview was first broadcast on CBC Radio's "Writers & Company" and produced by Lisa Godfrey.

WACHTEL: You often write about characters who live between cultures, and much of your novel, *The Farming of Bones*, takes place, literally, on a border: the river separating Haiti from the Dominican Republic. This is a place with a tragic history. Can you talk about what happened there in 1937?

DANTICAT: 1937 was a time of several dictators. In the Dominican Republic, Rafael Trujillo was running things, and he ordered a massacre of cane workers. By most accounts, this was ordered by him and carried out by his soldiers, and the massacre was aimed at Haitian workers. It was feared, at that time that, perhaps because of past history—Haiti occupied the Dominican Republic for twenty-two years—that this was about to happen again. And when the sugar-cane industry shifted from Cuba to the Dominican Republic, and a large number of people went to work there, there was this sense of a cultural invasion. And so, General Trujillo ordered this massacre in which anywhere from fifteen to forty thousand people were killed.

WACHTEL: So he was fearing a kind of Fifth Column or something, that these Haitians would take over the country?

DANTICAT: It was more a fear that people would quickly inter-marry, and it was even stated that he was afraid that, within three generations, the Dominican Republic would become much more like Haiti than its own self.

WACHTEL: You've said that it was your own visit to the Massacre River that inspired you to write fictionally about that genocide. What did you find there?

DANTICAT: I think it was what I *didn't* find there that most moved me. I had read so much about the Massacre River, going from the first massacre of the colonists in the nineteenth century to this present massacre. And I think I had built up in my mind this angry, raging river, this body of water that just did not forget. And I felt that, as soon as I got there, I would sense the history, that I would see it as though unfolding on a screen. But when I got there, it amazed me that there were people washing clothes, that there were children bathing, that there were animals drinking. The ordinariness of life was striking to me. There's a line in the book that says that "Nature has no memory," and it struck me in a great sense that it's both sad and comforting that nature has no memory, that things go on in spite of what's happened before. That the trees will grow, that there will be weeds and that the river will flow. So, it was the lack of event there that inspired me, that made me want to recall the past and write about this historical moment.

WACHTEL: How did you first hear about it?

DANTICAT: I knew about it since childhood, because I had many childhood friends in the neighbourhood where I grew up who had fathers, mothers, uncles, relatives who had gone over to work in the cane in the Dominican Republic. It's a very big industry that always requires workers, and many Dominicans don't want to work in the cane because there's a stigma to it, and so Haitians are heavily recruited to do the work. And many of them do not come back; people get caught in a series of debts, some people sell everything they have to go there, and they're ashamed to come back.

WACHTEL: Your narrator, Amabelle, is a young Haitian woman, a house-servant on a sugar-cane plantation in the Dominican Republic. And despite the evidence and despite the worries of her Haitian lover, she ignores the rumours of violence until it's almost too late. Beyond the dramatic value of that, why did you want to see history through Amabelle's initially disbelieving eyes?

DANTICAT: I personally have always been extremely fascinated by narrations of history through one voice. Anne Frank's telling of the Holocaust and Elie Wiesel's, all the different individual voices that, in some ways, can tell the larger story. But Amabelle's character is based on an actual story that I had heard, of a woman who worked all her life in the home of a military man, a colonel, and this woman, while serving supper, was stabbed at the dinner table by her employer. I knew that I wanted to write about someone like that who was sort of treading, as you said earlier, who was working these borders, these social borders, who knew both sides and felt like, somehow, she belonged to both sides but really didn't. I wanted to write about someone like that, but I wanted her to tell the story. I wanted her to live.

WACHTEL: One of the rumours that Amabelle dismisses seems almost too bizarre to be true, but it *is* true and this is where Dominicans are identifying and killing Haitians by testing their pronunciation of the word *parsley*.

DANTICAT: Yes, it's one of those things that you couldn't make up. I think one thing that General Trujillo realized—he had also worked as a guard in a sugar-cane field earlier in his life—he realized that language, like anything else, can be a border. You couldn't tell exactly who was who just by looking at people. So they would ask people to say certain words, and one of the words was *perejil*, which is the word for *parsley*, and parsley is something that we use, that Haitians use, as a healing remedy, especially with matters of the blood. You drink the tea to cleanse the blood, you cleanse the dead, a cleansing herb. And, in this case, it was so abundant and so familiar that people were asked to say it. And if you're a Creole speaker, you don't roll your *R* the same way, and he knew that, he knew all the subtleties and the nuances of language, and that's what was used to test people, to see on which side they belonged.

WACHTEL: But that must be particularly potent to a writer, the idea that language itself can save or kill you.

DANTICAT: Rita Dove has a wonderful poem, "Parsley," where she writes about that and she approaches it as a bird call, and the General is teaching his birds to trill an *R* as he is plotting this massacre. It was very haunting and poignant as I was writing. And there were all these languages at play, there was Creole, there was Spanish, and there was English that I was writing in, so there was an echo to it sometimes that was very daunting.

WACHTEL: Your epigraph is from the Bible, from Judges.

DANTICAT: Actually someone found that for me and I was really blown away by it because it *shows* you that sometimes we can make up these borders. I've heard from some Dominican friends that now, often in U.S. customs, they will stop them and ask them to say words that they say differently than Puerto Ricans. It's

used as an immigration tool. So it continues. There are words that can betray you, words that can give you away. You can only pass so much until you open your mouth and then the words can betray you.

WACHTEL: And the Bible story that you quoted refers to the men of Gilead trying to cross over and they're tested by how they say the word *Shibboleth*.

DANTICAT: Yes. It says a lot about how circular these stories are, how circular life is.

WACHTEL: Tell me about the title of your novel, *The Farming of Bones*, because it too has a number of meanings.

DANTICAT: Well, "the farming of bones," the first source of it, comes from my conversations with people who work in the cane. I love Haitian art, and I've written a lot about it, particularly what is called "naïve" art, like the little detail from the painting that's on the book jacket. Often in that art is a representation of people cutting cane. And it's so beautifully done, the cutters are choreographed and the cane is gorgeous, and I was once talking to a man about that and I said, "If you object to this representation of what you do, how would you paint it, how would you describe it?" And he told me, "I work the land, I'm working the land to grow bones." A couple of weeks after I was flipping through a book of poetry by Pablo Neruda and came across this line, this verse, where he says, in translation he says "It is, at this stage, too late for a beginning, but this is my feeling, that nothing can silence me but death and its plows for the farming of bones." So it just seemed to cohere somehow, these two things. The phrase talks about the futility of the work, but also, in this case, the death that it brings to so many people who are involved in it at that time.

WACHTEL: Language and identity are central to your fiction as, in a way, they have been in your life. You live in the United States but you grew up in Haiti until you were twelve. Can you tell me about the place where you lived there?

DANTICAT: My parents left when I was young and left me with my aunt and uncle, and we spent our time between the city where they lived and the provinces in summer for vacation. So, I was spending almost the same amount of time every year in a very rural setting up in the mountains where you walked for hours to get there after you got dropped off by the car, and also in the city. I grew up between those two spaces, knowing people who, like my uncle, had travelled, who had been here and to the United States, and other people who had never left the place on the hill where they were born. It is a combination of both things which make up the reality of Haiti.

WACHTEL: How were you affected by the fact that your parents had already gone to America and

you were farmed out to different parts of the family?

DANTICAT: It was hard to feel bad about it. I missed them terribly, I missed my parents, but I was pretty young when they left and I had this very large surrogate family that was doting and took care of me and my brother. But it was very hard to feel terrible because people would always tell us how lucky we were because we were surrounded by people even poorer than we were. We were always told, "Your mother is in New York, your father is in New York, you get to go to school." We got to go to school. We never missed school because our parents were working to send money for it every month, and there was always that hope that they were going to send for us. So, there was a sense that we were kind of special. I think later, when you get older, you deal with the absences and you realize that there are things that you missed that you're trying to catch up on.

WACHTEL: In your first novel, *Breath, Eyes, Memory*, your Haitian narrator, Sophie, has a mother who emigrates to the United States and leaves her behind with an aunt. I'm not suggesting that it's autobiographical, but you describe so movingly in that novel the moment that Sophie has to leave Haiti to join her mother, and I wondered, do you remember how you felt when you were twelve?

DANTICAT: Oh, absolutely. I mean, I think Sophie's leaving is wrought with more political things surrounding it, but I definitely remember the emotional pull and tug, the feeling of being steeped in loyalties between the family that had taken care of you and the family that was truly your blood family, your mother and father, now going to rejoin them. I definitely felt that tug and the fear of "where would I fit in to this?" I had a space, at least, in my surrogate family that was established, but where would I fit in in this new family? I had two brothers who

were born in America who we hadn't seen, except once when they were babies when my parents brought them, and so there was a lot of uncomfortableness about starting a new life. And not just even thinking about the new life in the way when you go to a new place when you're an adult, but really surrendering because there's nothing that you can do for yourself at this stage in the beginning. So all of those feelings I knew and still remember very vividly, and I used that and the emotions to tell Sophie's story.

WACHTEL: Surrendering. That's an interesting word.

DANTICAT: Well, I think adults do it, too. I think it's probably more tragically painful to people who were independent linguistically, independent in other ways, to come to a new country and suddenly to be led places. It's scary all around. People say that immigration infantilizes people. And the older you get, the more you appreciate how brave people are to just leave some place without any knowledge of what it's going to be like, just knowing that it might be a little better than what you're leaving, and to just *arrive* and not speak the language. It's an enormous leap of faith, and I have a great deal of respect for people who do it.

WACHTEL: The idea of infantilizing people sounds accurate, and I wonder whether children are slightly more resilient because they're not that far from being in that state of helplessness.

DANTICAT: And thus the surrender. I think, when you're a child, you're more used to surrendering.

WACHTEL: You also write very movingly about Sophie's love for the aunt who raises her. This is in your novel *Breath, Eyes, Memory*. Did you experience that kind of bond with your surrogate family?

DANTICAT: I think that that kind of bond is inevitable because there is a deep void that exists when suddenly you're without your mother and your father. And it's even deeper than not ever having had one because, if you are adopted at birth, you've not known anything else, and so this is your family. And later you ask questions. But I think that if suddenly you feel like your parents are plucked from you, there's a void and you look for people to fill it. I had very close relationships with my aunt and my uncle because I was looking for them to be the parents, to be a kind of emotional source of parenting for me, to love me like my mother would have. So I think there's a really strong bond. My mother still says "You have your other sets of parents who are in Haiti."

WACHTEL: Did the sense of community among Haitians in New York help you out?

DANTICAT: It helped a lot in the transition and I think, even with the adults, that helps—having a transition, having a bridge, people who carry you over while you're adjusting to the new place. So that was very important to me, having the church that we went to on Sunday and the people who lived in our building. It was like a little village. We looked after other people's children and they looked after our children. There was a sense of community. You didn't feel so anonymous, you didn't feel so stranded, and I know this was a big concern to my parents that if something happened to you, there was somebody you could call who could come within seconds, who lived next door, who lived down the street. It was very important.

WACHTEL: When you were still in Haiti, you grew up during the regime of Baby Doc Duvalier. You were very young, but do you remember the ways it affected life in Haiti during the 1970s?

DANTICAT: A lot of us *must* remember. I remember a great deal of silence, people being afraid to say anything. You didn't trust your neighbour because you didn't know who might turn you in for whatever reason. And I remember them driving by in a limousine and throwing money out on the street and people just climbing on top of each other to get it. And they would do it on holidays, especially on the first of the year, the second of the year, which is a traditional time where you get money from your godparents or presents for the year. And so, things like that, throwing people a bone . . . right now there's a very strange nostalgia for that, I think. There's a proverb that says "Yesterday is always better," but it was a really difficult time. A lot of people would just vanish overnight or they would go into exile or would run. It was a difficult time. It's a difficult time right now, but it's difficult for other reasons.

WACHTEL: And, back then, were you aware it was a bone, were you aware that it was a dangerous place?

DANTICAT: I don't think I was aware. It's funny because, when we would have adults who would *visit* us in America—for example from Haiti later on in the last years of the dictatorship—there were things that you would hear that had happened in Haiti, demonstrations and so on, that they didn't hear when they were *there* because the media was so controlled. So I don't think I was aware either. I think I just thought that's how everybody lived, there was just this normal state. But there were precautions you took. You never spoke politics to anybody, you tried to stay out of things. I think that people developed survival mechanisms and, whether you were young or you were old, you developed certain codes, you just picked up what you should do and what you shouldn't do.

WACHTEL: You spoke Creole at home with your family, but French was the official language at school. Did that seem odd?

DANTICAT: It didn't seem odd. Again, you know, that was just how it was and that's how it is still for a lot of places. I mean, we spoke Creole at home, but the teacher, if you spoke Creole, would say, "Rephrase that." But that's changing somewhat now. They have Creole schools where they teach Creole and French together, because French remains a language of access for a lot of people, so it's not completely dismissed. I never felt as comfortable in French as I did in Creole, but there were things you just imagined "Okay, this is how it is" and we tried to make the best of it in the situation.

WACHTEL: Did that mean that Creole had a certain context or certain associations for you because it wasn't the official language?

DANTICAT: It felt, and it still feels sometimes, more intimate. But, for me, it didn't feel bad, it didn't feel like something unsavoury or anything, it just felt like this is what we speak when we're together and then, when you're at the bank or at the hospital, this is the public language, this is what shows your schooling. It's very much the same, for example, with, say, if you're in Jamaica with the Jamaican patois or the King's English and all the different social associations that people make with the different ways that people speak.

WACHTEL: And then you come to New York at twelve and they speak English.

DANTICAT: Yes, exactly. And the people, at least, who were around us, who were mostly working class people, a lot of them wouldn't speak much

French. We would just speak Creole in our space. If you wanted to participate in the dialogue of the world and understand what was going on, we were all doing our best to speak English.

WACHTEL: In *Breath, Eyes, Memory*, Sophie, unlike you, arrives in New York to find a mother who is really suffering. I mean, she's well-intentioned but she's having a very hard time. What did you want to explore or why did you want to explore this kind of imperiled mother/daughter relationship?

DANTICAT: I wanted to explore the ways that a young girl would become a woman on her own, without much modeling, without perfect modeling. I wanted to explore how we become women in the absence of our mothers. And the rites of passage to womanhood. I wanted to experience the whole range of womanhood. From a woman whose family, and this particular family, has that obsession with virginity, to being raped, to all the relationships between women in the family and to women outside the family, and to the family traditions and legacies. The way they identify themselves, both alone and in association with their family relationships. I wanted to explore all of that and how that's affected by migration. I think, with migration, when we come to a new country, we all come with fragments. When you leave, you take what you can—you take some pictures, you take your stories, you take your memories, and the rest

you feel like you can get better, and more of, in the other place. You can get better apples, you can get better bananas. But your memories, you can't get better memories. They just stay. And so, I just wanted to explore how a young woman would put all those fragments together and do it on her own because her mother's rite of passage was this violent act, which was true for a lot of women who lived in the dictatorship.

WACHTEL: Sophie's mother was raped and, in fact, Sophie herself is the result of that rape.

DANTICAT: Yes. And so, as she says in the story, she has to put all these different fragments together to create a face for herself, just to imagine what her father would look like and taking what's already there of her mother. So everything is a puzzle. It's almost as if, when she's taken out of where she was and she's in a new place, she has to reform herself, she has to recreate a self that can survive in this place. The mother never learns that, and that's what she succumbs to.

WACHTEL: There is this darker side, as well. You say you not only wanted to explore the obsession with virginity but also the violence of rape. Tell me about the obsession with virginity, because you talk about it being a rural Haitian tradition, to physically test a daughter's virginity.

DANTICAT: It's true for some Haitian women, it's not true for *all* Haitian women. But it is something that happens in *this* family. You find often in stratified societies that poor women are encouraged to be marriageable. And especially in this rural setting, this family, not having a father, the mother would have to be all the more forceful, all the more strict, with her daughter so that people could respect them. So, the grandmother checks this and that, she wants them to remain virgins so that they can be respected and marry well, and I don't think that's a tradition that's unique to Haitian culture. A lot of people who read the book from different cultures, a lot of women would say their mothers had taken them to doctors, for instance. There's this sense of honour, and as the mother says, "If you die, you die alone, but if you dishonour yourself, you dishonour all of us." And in these very small, close communities, things like marriage are not between two people, it's between two families. And so, just working with all that and how those things transform, the grandmother, then, has this conversation with this daughter who lives in a new world and is trying to shape a new identity for herself. Will she take these things with her, and all the things we carry? I really wanted to play with that in terms of what that means, specifically, to women, especially women whose mothers and grandmothers are just trying to recreate these customs and trying to stay the same in this new place, which is virtually impossible.

WACHTEL: But you got some criticism from Haitian-Americans for writing about that.

DANTICAT: Well, absolutely, because it wasn't true for all of them, so then people would say, "You're lying, you're making this up," and I said, "Well, you know, it's fiction, you can lie in fiction." But it was true for some people, it was true for some women who did share their stories. But their voices, of course, are not louder than the people who are protesting. But I think it is important to have a dialogue, and not to condemn anything, but to really have a dialogue about how we are transformed by migration and how much of the things that were useful to us, say, where my parents were born, are useful here. A lot of them are, a lot of them I carry with me, a lot of them are part of me, but some of them aren't anymore. What I try to do is get closer to the experiences, not really offer solutions. But I think sometimes, when you're writing about a community, some people from that community may feel you are betraying them, that you're putting on a show for the mainstream or that you're ratting or that you're just not being a good compatriot in some way.

WACHTEL: You've had to bear a lot of responsibility because you're the first woman from Haiti to write in English in America. I mean, that's been sort of loaded on you whether you like it or not.

DANTICAT: There have been some others and there are more coming up, and I can't wait, because it's a very uncomfortable space between both communities. Some people think that you're a native informant, that what you say must be true even though it's fiction. So I'm really excited to see more people coming and I can't wait until there are at least twenty of us.

WACHTEL: You called your short story collection *Krik Krak*. Can you talk about what that expression means?

DANTICAT: "Krik krak" is a call-and-response that we do before telling riddles or telling stories. It's an introduction to the storytelling if you have an audience in front of you, and it's usually an exchange between an elder and some children, but it 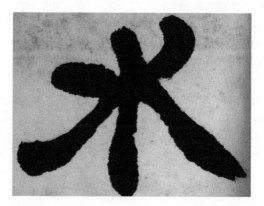 ranges. So the old man or woman will say "krik" and the children will say "krak," with much enthusiasm. And there's a lot of different combinations that we do to warm up the listener. So it's really one of the rare moments where people of extreme generations—you have the eldest people in the family and the youngest people in the family—are in an exchange that is really even, and they can exchange stories and they can laugh together. I wanted to name my short story collection for that tradition because I was told stories by my grandmothers and my aunts when I was young, and I felt like that was my first lesson

in narrative. The storyteller's very attuned to the audience, and if the children are yawning then they'll sing a song. There's a lot of interaction. So I called it that to honour this tradition of storytelling and my past and my life.

WACHTEL: In your fiction, you'll have dreams or symbols or even visitations from the dead or the world of the spirit bump into the harshest realities, and I was just wondering, is this something that was in the folktales and the stories that you heard in childhood?

DANTICAT: One of the things about the folktale is that so much is possible. Fish can fly and butterflies can sing and I think that's very liberating to the imagination of a child, the fact that another world exists. But also, not to make it sound too mystical, that there are more possibilities, the world is more than what we see. For example, if you're sitting in a room and there's a big draft, then you might think *ah, someone's come to visit.* That would be the first thing that would pop in my mind; not everyone who is Haitian would think that, but that was part of my reality.

WACHTEL: In one of the stories in *Krik Krak*, a story called "1937," a woman's mother is accused of being a witch. She's supposed to have flown to safety from the Dominican Republic across the river into Haiti, and for this she's imprisoned as a witch. Can you talk about the spiritual dimension in that story, because there's also a mix—there's a Madonna, a Catholic element as well.

DANTICAT: I grew up hearing stories about these women who fly and, if you were a child, you were supposed to avoid them. You don't go out at night because there are women who fly who are not good to children. And they have these wings of flames, and I remember hearing that when I was young and I just thought, "God, I'd just love to see one," but if you see one, you don't live. And there were women who were arrested for sorcery, and people could accuse them if something happened to their child, and that still happens in some cases. During the dictatorship for example, François Duvalier, Papa Doc, used some of that. He called his personal security force, the Volunteers for National Security, *les Tontons Macoutes*. When you were growing up you were told that, if you were bad, the *macoute* would come for you, it's like a bogeyman in the night. And he had just taken that and brought it alive, sort of a nation's nightmare alive. There were so many places where the scary story worked into your life. I wanted to play with some of that in the way that I had experienced it, both with African religion and with Catholicism. Ultimately, if there are women who truly fly, of course, their wings will be clipped. I wanted to play with the very narrow space where the reality and the fantasy clash against each other in real life.

WACHTEL: Even though it was your grandmother and aunts who told stories, you once said, "In Haitian culture, women are taught to be silent. But I must write." Why was it that very silence that made the need so urgent?

DANTICAT: I don't know. And now I'm thinking, "Did I say that?" I must have been brazen in some point of my life. I just wrote a foreword for a book of testimony of the women who were victims under the coup recently in 1993, and a lot of the women are telling testimonies about what happened to them—many of them were raped, and they go through all this struggle, some of them were beaten and went to prison—and now they're telling their stories, and there's a sense that you must tell where it might be better for you to be silent or, if you're raped, your husband might leave you. And that's not specific to Haitian culture, you know, that whole worry about stirring things up. But, I think, in the face of the silence that came before, there is that feeling that if you have a voice, you must speak.

WACHTEL: But women in particular?

DANTICAT: Women in particular because our society is like other societies where women, especially poor women, are not often given the opportunity to speak. Other people speak for them. Which is why I always say that I don't want to be called anybody's voice because, I think, if you are somebody's voice, you render them voiceless. I want everybody to have the opportunity to speak. But I think particularly poor women are always . . . they're there, but other people are speaking for them, their men speak for them, other women who are better educated or better off speak for them.

WACHTEL: You have a piece in *Krik Krak* in which a mother is disappointed and worried that her daughter has chosen writing. Did your own mother have problems with your deciding to be a writer?

DANTICAT: Well, my mother was, and I think still is, nervous for me about my being a writer, and part of it comes from our legacy in that, most of the people who were writing in my mother's lifetime in Haiti in her youth were in prison or exiled. And even in my time, if anybody wrote anything contrary to the official line, they were put in prison or they were sent away or they were killed. So it wasn't the best career choice, you know. With the sacrifices of the immigration experience—so much is given up for you, so much is sacrificed—it's expected that you will do something sane and predictably stable. So I wasn't encouraged to pursue this life.

WACHTEL: And even now?

DANTICAT: Now, for me, I'm thinking I need a back-up. There's a proverb that says you don't step in the river with both feet, you test it with one foot, so you're always testing. But I think there's this sense that you have to make good, you have to do well, you can't blow the life that was sacrificed for you or the things that were done for you. But my mother's hesitation about me being a writer is primarily political, the personal risk and the political risk, and all the things that a young woman, as she would put it, risks in just being out there and saying things that might offend people. The confrontational element of doing this work echoes, for her, back from when she was growing up with it and with the legacy of the writers we have. Many of our writers were martyred, and so that comes into play.

WACHTEL: You visit Haiti quite often. In fact, you were there quite recently. What is it like for you now?

DANTICAT: I have come to terms with the fact that my relationship with Haiti is different than someone who lives there, than it is for my uncle and aunt and others who live there. But I love being there. There's a kind of peace about it that I can't explain. But I realize also that I'm not living, I'm staying for a certain period of time, at the end of which I travel back. And so, it's a relationship of insider/outsider. Being in, I feel, my soul feels, a kind of unrest and I wish that things were better. There is a point in my life when I will go back, I feel, but it's still a developing relationship. There are so many people that, even with the way things are, plan to go back. People like my parents' generation always planned to go back, and then the dictatorship went on for thirty years and they couldn't go back. But there is that pull for me, a sense that there are many times when I feel that this is where I belong, but I don't want to go back and be part of the problem. I have to find a way that I can serve first, and be there in a way that's healing for me and healing for the place at the same time. So I'm still processing my returns every time I go. It stirs a lot of emotions, and gets me thinking about a lot of things when I'm there.

WACHTEL: There's an old Haitian song that you quote in a story in *Krik Krak* where the lyrics say "Beloved Haiti, there's no place like you. I had to leave you before I could understand you." Do you relate to that sentiment?

DANTICAT: It's ironic because when you get off the plane in Port Au Prince, usually there's a band singing that song. So everybody who goes back hears that song, because it is so true. Probably, if I moved from the United States and went to live somewhere else, I would see America differently too. I think there's a kind of stepping out of the self, and I thank God that things are better, I'm happy that things are a little better now, that people can go back, and that you can have that relationship of stepping back. It's sort of a restructuring of home and reclaiming, but reclaiming in a different way, humbly, just going as an insider/outsider, stepping one foot in the river, one foot at a time.

WACHTEL: Haiti is a country with such a history of poverty and violence. Do Haitians see their country as a tragic place?

DANTICAT: I don't think people see it as a tragic place. I think if things were better, if things were, say, thirty per cent better, most people would not leave. And you can judge from the number of people who, after forty years in the United States, are still dreaming of going back. People are forced to leave, and it's tragic to them to have to leave, young people especially, who, after trying and trying, feel like they have to emigrate to make it. That I find tragic, and a lot of people inside find that tragic, that the people who could be building it have to leave in order to survive. So I don't think they see the *place* as tragic, I think they see the circumstances, the destiny we've had, the mismanagement, the bad leadership at times, as tragic.

Bringing Tony Home

by Tissa Abeysekara

MICHAEL ONDAATJE

WHEN I READ *Bringing Tony Home* three years ago, it felt as if I had come across a book from my childhood, one I already knew well. It was of course my childhood I had come across, found evoked—with that strange, exaggerated sense of description ("as the woman disappeared inside the house I noticed she was frighteningly thin and flat, like a steamroller had gone over her"), and with an enlarged sense of things, such as a too-heavy jug one was supposed to carry a great distance. There was too the delicious and sad sense of being solitary in the world, with a thousand intricacies between you and your closest neighbour or relative.

In the last years of the forties, when I had still not reached ten years of age, my family became desperately poor.

So begins *Bringing Tony Home*.

The author, Tissa Abeysekara, is a contemporary Sri Lankan filmmaker who in mid-life wrote this first novella or memoir about a disappearing moment from his childhood. It is a book written by someone roughly my age, about a mutual era of childhood. I had, till reading it, never found a book with such a physical echo of my life in Sri Lanka. Usually I transpose the location and setting in any novel about childhood that I read so I can fit the events into a familiar place. For instance, as a boy in Sri Lanka I knew only one house that had a staircase and so for many years whenever anyone in a novel climbed or descended the stairs, whether a Karamazov or the Count of Monte Cristo, they did so in my Aunt Nedra's house.

So Tissa Abeysekara's slim novel about a childhood loss took me right to the place of my youth. Not just to Sri Lanka, not just to Colombo, but specifically to the High Level Road in Boralesgamuwa. And there, in a place I knew and could recognize—and could slip into without translation—I was introduced to the people in his boyhood story, coloured and altered by the forty years of the author's adult life.

It is a simple story about a family that has to leave a district because of a change in their fortunes and must leave behind the family dog. The boy, a week later, returns on his own to the village to look for "Tony," and because of the narrator's smallness, and because of the "largeness" of the world around him, the journey he makes is mythic. "The glass smelled vaguely of sardine and the water tasted like when it is taken from a galvanized bucket, but I drank it all in one breath and returned the glass to the woman with both hands. . . ." I feel that already I am simplifying a privately-heard tale. It is a book I wish to share only by passing it over to a reader. Funny and tender. Dangerous. Unfair. And of course it is one of the saddest stories.

What is wonderful is the way Tissa Abeysekara can make a whole era hang on a single strand of memory:

> Each year during the April season a giant wheel would be constructed in Depanama and it would be there till after Wesak; this year they were constructing it on the little hill overlooking the Pannipitiya Railway Station where, once-upon-a-time there was a tennis court and every Saturday Father would come in the evening to play tennis with Messrs. Arthur Kotelawela, Bulner, Subasingha, and the Station Master, Mr Samarasinha, and I would sit perched on the embankment by the cactus bushes with Guneris the servant boy and watch the trains come and go in the station below, and during the Sri Pada season, which was from early January to late May, the trains were full of pilgrims and white cloth fluttered like bird feathers from the windows, sheaths of areacanut pods bristled, voices chanted and along with it the iron wheels of the train braked, clanged and screeched, all blending together in perfect harmony and held together by the sad melancholy whistle of the train as it left the station and behind was the sound of the tennis ball hitting the racquet, the ground or the net in a soft but clear and varying rhythm. . . .
>
> Then one by one they stopped playing; Mr Subasingha disappeared because—I heard my Mother and Father whispering to each other— his wife had run away with a Tamil gentleman who was the Apothecary at the local government dispensary; Mr. Kotelawela had a stroke and was ordered complete rest; the Station Master, Mr Samarasinha started drinking during the day also and was too drunk by evening to play tennis, and old Mr. Bulner simply stopped playing. We moved from the big house to the small one at Depanama and Father had no time to play for he left early in the morning on a bicycle and would return late at night even on Saturdays, and sometimes he would be gone for days. And the tennis court was abandoned and weeds grew all over it

and the iron roller that used to level the court was dragged by some village boys to the top of the little hill and rolled down where it ended in a ditch and lay there like a broken animal.

The portrait of the world is farcical and formal in the way the author insists on giving us a torrent of details and names and everyone's official role, for children know and remember the labels on adults: the Station Master, an Apothecary. And it is these details of society in his memory, "blending together in perfect harmony" that once held his childhood together. Eventually the habits of parents, the memories of public fights, are discovered to be mutable. So it is a book not just of a child dealing with the loss of one dear dog but of everything, the whole world that surrounds his life. This is why the descriptions are detailed and appear to be frantic, an aria of lists which tries to hold the past together.

The tragedy within the book is not the loss of the animal but the boy's awareness that he must in the end leave it. He is being forced to turn into an adult. This is the deeper sadness in this story. On a second reading we realise the boy in the story is looking back, he is ahead of us, so that contemporary opinions and events also flood in within this "slight" story being told in double time, with young and with ancient eyes:

By eleven o'clock I had finished my assignments: rations from the coop store—the smelly yellowy big-grained milchard, six chundus of it at two per coupon, sugar, brown sticky and smelling faintly like stale bees' honey, three

pounds of it; Dhal, the variety referred to as "Mysoor parippu," fine-grained and pink and mistakenly believed to be coming from Mysore in India and boycotted under the orders of the JVP when the Indian Peace Keeping Force was alleged to be raping girls in Jaffna in the late eighties until someone enlightened us that the dhal had nothing to do with India and was really "Masoor Dhal" which came from Turkey. . . .

We hold onto favourite books for reasons that are not universal. Each word and sentence in this one carried me into arms I'd been in before. No other book brings me as close to my lost self.
It is a lost classic for me, too, because of the book's quick fate. Published in Sri Lanka by a small press, it has so far not been published anywhere else. It was a story written far from the publishing centres of the west and there it remains, still lost to the rest of the world.

The Lover
of the Hummingbird

"Remembering The Passion Artist: John Hawkes Tribute,"
April 13, 1999, Brown University

JEFFREY EUGENIDES

TWENTY YEARS AGO I arrived on this campus intent on fulfilling my father's greatest fear—while making him pay for it—of having his son ruined by the liberal Eastern Establishment. At the time I didn't know what the liberal Eastern Establishment was. Its major recommendation lay in my father's opposition to it. If I'd been asked to describe this group, I would have offered only superficial details: the wrinkled broadcloth shirts, the flood pants, the Latinate vocabulary, the lock-jaw speech.

I had chosen Brown chiefly because of the presence on its faculty of one John Hawkes. Hawkes's books, which I only dimly understood, had enchanted me ever since I'd pulled my first copy off a high school teacher's bookshelf when I was fifteen. I don't want to be hyperbolic about the moment but it retains in memory all the annunciatory trumpets of an epiphany. I can remember reading the words "New Directions" on the spine. I can remember studying the picture on the cover of a muscular, nearly anatomized Carribean woman posed before a blazing sun. Most of all, I remember the intoxicating effect the prose had on me, like a dangerous throat-burning Scandinavian liqueur. The narrative voice seized me in a way all the noisy art forms of the time (which have only grown noisier since then) somehow didn't. I felt right away, reading the first paragraph of *Second Skin*, that I was in the presence of the qualities Nabokov considered the hallmarks of art: curiosity, tenderness, kindness, ecstasy.

I set out on my pilgrimage my first day here on College Hill. Consulting my campus map, I located Horace Mann. I studied the directory inside the door. With mounting excitement I climbed the steps. Everything was old in the way I wanted it to be. The stairs creaked; the radiators gave off a smell of rust, the smell of the Ivy League, which I inhaled deeply as I searched for the right room. At the end of the hall, in a forlorn office clearly used for perhaps three hours each semester, sat a man with owl-shaped eyeglasses the colour of congealed honey. He looked up at me.

"Are you the lover of the hummingbird?" I asked.

And in that unmistakable voice, putting aside his insistence that you should never confuse a novel's author with its protagonist (because he could see that such a distinction would have been lost on the kid in his doorway), Professor Hawkes answered in the affirmative.

And so it was that Jack Hawkes became for me the living embodiment of the Liberal Eastern Elite. It turned out they didn't wear broadcloth shirts. They wore navy blue or white turtlenecks, chinos and tweed jackets. They didn't speak in lock-jaws but in a voice, well, like Jack's, something between the cry of an eagle and the whine of a very intelligent bookish asthmatic child . . . you all know the voice, you can hear it now, saying the things Jack used to say. "But what about the character's eyes? Look how the author describes his eyes. These aren't eyes. They're gonads! In Freudian terms the eye is always a gonad!"

Or when he forgot somebody's name: "It's the synapses!"

Or regarding literary poseurs: "To glorify not the writing but the writer, to be concerned with the role of the writer in society rather than the work itself, that is something which, I must say, I strongly resist."

This last remark was delivered to me. Because pretty soon in our dealings with each other Jack realized that my interest in him extended beyond my admiration for his books. One day during my freshman year I came into class and sat next to Jack. I bent over to lay my books on the floor. While I was down there, though, I took the opportunity to stare under Jack's seat.

In an instant Jack was shouting. "You even want to know what kind of shoes I wear?"

I was horrified at being caught, at having my idolatry exposed. I blushed and sat back in my seat and tried from then on not even to look at Jack's shoes.

Among my pitiful efforts that first semester in Beginning Fiction, I remember one moment when Jack gave me encouragement, a memory still more dear to me than any subsequent praise or favorable review. We were given an assignment to describe a single mundane moment with utmost dramatic effect. I had described—taxidermied, really—a little girl in the act of turning on a light switch. But generous Jack found some promise.

"I love this little girl," he shouted. "I want to eat this girl!"

That was a lesson I've never forgotten: try to make every page of prose edible.

AMONG THE MOST EDIBLE pages in our literature surely are those written by John Hawkes. Open any book, anywhere, and the feast is laid out before you. I've always agreed with Proust's insistence that you can measure a writer's talent from any paragraph in any book. Just for fun, in preparing these remarks, I opened a few of Jack's books at random. From The Cannibal: "And old Herman, fully awake, touched the soft fur with his mouth, and felt the wings through the cotton dress, while in the far end of town, a brigade of men passed shallow buckets of water to quench a small fire." From The Blood Oranges : "I swayed, I listened, I shaded my eyes, knowing that Catherine was indeed asleep and that Fiona's haste was justified but futile and that the light itself had turned to wind or that the wind had somehow assumed the properties of the dawn light." From Sweet William: "There I was, standing on racing turf at last. Through the shredding curtains of that brisk dawn mirage, a fusion of fog and filmy light and dark shadows, I was able to make out the quarters of the track, as well as the darkened shape of the grandstand, which was like an abandoned ship on its side."

Not only was Jack a wonderful writer; he was a truly first-rate hypochondriac. "Nobody has a cold, do they?" was his usual greeting to our class. If a sufferer were identified, Jack quarantined the poor student in a remote armchair before administering himself the booster vaccine of a glass of Soave Folonari. Of course Jack had had asthma since childhood and needed to guard against flus and colds. And, having done some teaching now myself, I understand the temptation to view stu-

dents less as presidential material than viral. Nevertheless, one of the strangest things I ever learned about Jack, and something that impressed upon me the mysteriousness of human character (another literary lesson, I suppose), was the following. One of the last times I saw Jack, at a lunch with Rick Moody, Jack, a man who had fled the slight-

Jacqueline Rau, *Nu*, 1938

est cough or sniffle, calmly mentioned over a rich dessert that doctors had just determined that his main cardiac arteries were occluded by eighty or ninety percent. He seemed—and again I have only that one afternoon to go on—almost fascinated with the diagnosis, as though the heart condition in question was something he was thinking about giving to one of his characters. And so, to all the other qualities I admired about Jack Hawkes, I had to add another: courage.

That final lunch was not without its sadder aspects. Jack was concerned about his book, *The Frog*, which had come out that year. He was afraid it wasn't doing well enough to suit his publisher and he asked Rick and me if we thought there was anything we could do, down in New York, to give the book some added attention. It was an uncomfortable moment, which I can only compare, in my own experience, to the time my own father, late in life, asked to borrow money. It went against the natural order of things. And we were standing in the middle of a gravel parking lot, in Providence, which is always a sad thing, and Jack looked frail in the harsh light. But no sooner had this unease descended on us than Jack, synapses still intact, summed up the entire situation and, waving his hand, dismissed the whole idea.

In retrospect, I think he was stripping from himself the last shreds of the mantle I had forced on his shoulders so many years ago when I barged into his office quoting *Second Skin*. He was telling me that he was a writer and, like any writer, he worried about the fate of his books in the world. He was telling me, now that I was old enough to understand, exactly what kind of shoes he wore. And what kind of shoes, in emulating him, I had squeezed myself into.

It was my good fortune to study with the great cantankerous Hawkes and to know him as a teacher and as a friend, to enjoy his kindness and humour, his histrionic self-dramatizing, his pagan vitality, and to hear from his own lips the natural flow of his eloquence and the utterly original workings of his fine and incomparable mind.

When I graduated, I wrote a note of thanks to Jack, most of which I've forgotten. The last line, however, comes back to me. "I will always begin with what you taught me." That is as true today, as we gather here to celebrate the man and his work, as it was in 1983. I want to say, God Bless John Hawkes, but it doesn't feel right. Jack was an existentialist. He told me once that he liked the idea that we create our work out of the void. So rather than address Jack in heaven, I'll end by saluting the god he spoke of most often, the imagination, specifically the imagination of John Hawkes, which bodied forth from the void his many brilliant books.

Dense Clarity— Clear Density

WALTER MURCH

Simple and Complex

O NE OF THE DEEPEST impressions on someone who happens to wander into a film mixing studio is that there is no necessary connection between ends and means. Sometimes, to create the natural simplicity of an ordinary scene between two people, dozens and dozens of soundtracks have to be created and seamlessly blended into one. At other times an apparently complex "action" soundtrack can be conveyed with just a few carefully selected elements. In other words, it is not always obvious what it took to get the final result: it can be simple to be complex, and complicated to be simple. The general level of complexity, though, has been steadily increasing over the seven decades since film sound was invented. And starting with Dolby Stereo in the 1970s, continuing with computerized mixing in the 1980s and various digital formats in the 1990s, that increase has accelerated even further. Sixty years ago, for instance, it would not be unusual for an entire film to need only fifteen to twenty sound effects. Today that number could be hundreds to thousands of times greater.

Well, the film business is not unique: compare the single-take, single-track 78 rpm discs of the 1930s to the multiple-take, multi-track surround-sound CDs of today. Or look at what has happened with visual effects: compare King Kong of the 1930s to the Jurassic dinosaurs of the 1990s. The general level of detail, fidelity, and what might be called the "hormonal level" of sound and image has been vastly increased, but at the price of much greater complexity in preparation.

The consequence of this, for sound, is that during the final recording of almost every film there are moments when the balance of dialogue, music, and sound effects will suddenly (and sometimes unpredictably) turn into a logjam so extreme that even the most experienced of directors, editors, and mixers can be overwhelmed by the choices they have to make

I'd like to focus on these "logjam" moments: how they come about, and how to deal with them when they do. How to choose which sounds should predominate when they can't all be included? Which sounds should play second fiddle? And which sounds, if any, should be eliminated? As difficult as these questions are, and as vulnerable as such choices are to the politics of the filmmaking process, I'd like to suggest some conceptual and practical guidelines for threading your way through, and perhaps even disentangling, these logjams.

Or, better yet, not permitting them to occur in the first place.

Code and Body

TO BEGIN to get a handle on this, I'd like you to think about sound in terms of light.

White light, for instance, which looks so simple, is in fact a tangled superimposure of every wavelength (that is to say, every colour) of light simultaneously. You can observe this in reverse when you shine a flashlight through a prism and see the white beam fan out into the familiar rainbow of colours from violet (the shortest wavelength

of visible light) through indigo, blue, green, yellow, and orange to red (the longest wavelength).

Keeping this in mind, I'd now like you to imagine *white sound*—every imaginable sound heard together at the same time—the sound of New York City, for instance: cries and whispers, sirens and shrieks, motors, subways, jackhammers, street music, Grand Opera and Shea Stadium. Now imagine that you could "shine" this white sound through some kind of magic prism that would reveal to us its hidden spectrum.

Just as the spectrum of colours is bracketed by violet and red, this sound-spectrum will have its own brackets, or limits. Usually, in this kind of discussion, we would now start talking about the lowest audible (20 cycles) and highest audible (20,000 cycles) frequencies of sound. But for the purposes of our discussion I am going to ask you to imagine limits of a completely different conceptual order, something I'll call *Encoded* sound, which is analogous to the violet end of the light spectrum, and something else I'll call *Embodied* sound, which is analogous to the red end.

The clearest example of Encoded sound is *speech*.

The clearest example of Embodied sound is *music*.

When you think about it, every language is basically a code, with its own particular set of rules. You have to understand those rules in order to break open the husk of language and extract whatever meaning is inside. Just because we usually do this automatically, without realizing it, doesn't mean it isn't happening. It is happening right now, as you listen to this lecture. The meaning of what I am saying is "encoded" in the words I am using. Sound, in this case, is acting simply as a vehicle with which to deliver the code.

Music, however, is completely different: it is sound *experienced directly*, without any code intervening between you and it. Naked. Whatever meaning there is in a piece of music is "embodied" in the sound itself. This is why music is sometimes called the Universal Language.

What lies in between these outer limits? Just as every audible sound falls somewhere between the lower and upper limits of 20 and 20,000 cycles, so all sounds will be found somewhere on this conceptual spectrum from speech to music.

Most sound effects, for instance, fall midway: like "sound-centaurs," they are half language, half music. Since a sound effect usually refers to something specific—the steam engine of a train, the knocking at a door, the chirping of birds, the firing of a gun—it is not as "pure" a sound as music. But on the other hand, the language of

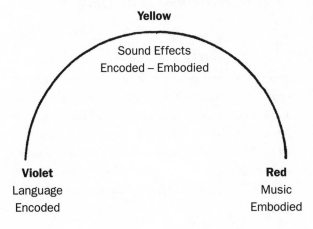

Yellow

Sound Effects
Encoded – Embodied

Violet
Language
Encoded

Red
Music
Embodied

sound effects, if I may call it that, is more universally and immediately understood than any spoken language.

Green and Orange

BUT NOW I'm going to throw you a curve (you expected this, I'm sure) and say that in practice things are not quite as simple as I have just made them out to be. There are musical elements that make their way into almost all speech—think of *how* someone says something as a kind of music. For instance, you can usually tell if someone is angry or happy, even if you don't understand what they are saying, just by listening to the tone—the music—of their voice. We understand R2D2 entirely through the music of his beeps and boops, not from his "words" (only C-3PO and Luke Skywalker can do that). Stephen Hawking's computerized speech, on the other hand, is perfectly understandable, but monotonously even—it has very little musical content—and so we have to listen carefully to *what* he says, not how he says it.

To the degree that speech has music in it, its "colour" will drift toward the warmer (musical) end of the spectrum. In this regard, R2D2 is warmer than Stephen Hawking, and Mr. Spock is cooler than Rambo.

By the same token, there are elements of code that underlie every piece of music. Just think of the difficulty of listening to Chinese Opera (unless you are Chinese!). If it seems strange to you, it is because you do not understand its code, its underlying assumptions. In fact, much of your taste in music is dependent on how many musical languages you have become familiar with, and how difficult those languages are. Rock and Roll has a simple underlying code (and a huge audience); modern European classical music has a complicated underlying code (and a smaller audience).

To the extent that this underlying code is an important element in the music, the "colour" of the music will drift toward the cooler (linguistic) end of the spectrum. Schönberg is cooler than Santana.

And sound effects can mercurially slip away from their home base of yellow toward either edge, tinting themselves warmer and more "musical," or cooler and more "linguistic" in the process. Sometimes a sound effect can be almost pure music. It doesn't declare itself openly *as music* because it is not melodic, but it can have a musical effect on you anyway: think of the dense ("orange") background sounds in Eraserhead. And sometimes a sound effect can deliver discrete packets of meaning that are almost like words. A door-knock, for instance, might be a "blue" micro-language that says: "Someone's here!" And certain kinds of footsteps say simply: "Step! Step! Step!"

Such distinctions have a basic function in helping you to classify—conceptually—the sounds for your film. Just as a well-balanced painting will have an interesting and proportioned spread of colours from complementary parts of the spectrum, so the sound-track of a film will appear balanced and interesting if it is made up of a well-proportioned spread of elements from our spectrum of "sound-colours."

I would like to emphasize, however, that these colours are completely independent of any emotional tone associated with "warmth" or "coolness." Although I have put music at the red (warm) end of the spectrum, a piece of music can be emotionally cool, just as easily as a line of dialogue—at the cool end of the spectrum—can be emotionally hot.

In addition, there is a practical consideration to all this when it comes to the final mix. It seems that the combination of certain sounds will take on a correspondingly different character depending on which part of the spectrum they come from—some sounds will superimpose transparently and effectively, whereas others will tend to interfere destructively with each other and "block up," creating a muddy and unintelligible mix.

Before we get into the specifics of this, though, let me say a few words about the differences of superimposing images and sounds.

Harmonic and Non-Harmonic

WHEN YOU LOOK at a painting or a photograph, or the view outside your window, you see distinct areas of colour—a yellow dress on a washing line, for instance, outlined against a blue sky. The dress and the sky occupy separate areas of the image. If they didn't—if the foreground dress was transparent—the wavelengths of yellow and blue would *add together* and create a new colour: green, in this case. This is just the nature of the way we perceive light.

You can superimpose *sounds*, though, and they still retain their original identity. The notes C, E, and G create something new: a harmonic C-major chord. But if you listen carefully you can still hear the original notes. It is as if, looking at something green, you still also could see the blue and the yellow that went into making it.

And it is a good thing that it works this way, because a film's soundtrack (as well as music itself) is utterly dependent on the ability of different sounds ("notes") to superimpose transparently upon each other, creating new "chords," without themselves being transformed into something totally different.

Are there limits to how much superimposure can be achieved?

Well, it depends on what we mean by superimposure. Every note played by every instrument is actually a superimposure of a series of tones. A cello playing "A," for instance, will vibrate strongly at that string's fundamental frequency, say 110 cycles per second. But the string also vibrates at exact multiples of that fundamental: 220, 330, 440, 550, 660, 770, 880, etc. These extra vibrations are called the *harmonic overtones* of the fundamental frequency.

Harmonics, as the name indicates, are sounds whose wave-forms are tightly linked—literally "nested" together. In the example above, 220, 440, and 880 are all higher octaves of the fundamental note "A" (110). And the other harmonics—330, 550, 660, and 770—correspond to the notes E, Db, E, and G which, along with A, are the four notes of the A-major chord (A-Db-E-G-A). So when the note A is played on the violin (or piano, or any other instrument), what you actually hear is a chord. But because the harmonic linkage is so tight, and because the fundamental (110 in this case) is almost twice as loud as all of its overtones put together, we perceive the "A" as a single note, albeit a note with "character." This character—or *timbre*—is slightly different for each instrument, and that difference is what allows us to distinguish not only between types of instrument—clarinets from violins, for example—but also sometimes between individual instruments of the same type—a Stradivarius violin from a Guarnieri.

This kind of *harmonic superimposure* has no practical limits to speak of. As long as the sounds are harmonically linked, you can superimpose as many elements as you want. Imagine an orchestra, with all the instruments playing octaves of the same note. Add an organ, playing more octaves. Then a chorus of two hundred, singing still more octaves. We are superimposing hundreds and hundreds of individual instruments and voices, but it will all still sound unified. If everyone started playing and singing whatever they felt like, however, that unity would immediately turn into chaos.

To give an example of non-musical harmonic superimposure: in *Apocalypse Now* we wanted to create the sound of a field of crickets for one of the beginning scenes (Willard alone in his hotel room at night), but for story reasons we wanted the crickets to have a hallucinatory degree of precision and focus. So rather than going out and simply recording a field of crickets, we decided to build

the sound up layer by layer out of individually recorded crickets. We brought a few of them into our basement studio, recorded them one by one on a multitrack machine, and then kept adding track after track, recombining these tracks and then recording even more until we had finally many thousands of chirps superimposed. The end result sounded unified—*a field* of crickets—even though it had been built up out of many individual recordings, because the basic unit (the cricket's chirp) is so similar—each chirp sounds pretty much like the last. This was not music, but it would still qualify, in my mind, as an example of harmonic superimposure.

(Incidentally, you'll be happy to know that the crickets escaped and lived happily behind the walls of this basement studio for the next few years, chirping at the most inappropriate moments.)

Dagwood and Blondie

WHAT HAPPENS, though, when the superimposure is not harmonic?

Technically, of course, you can superimpose as much as you want: you can create huge "Dagwood sandwiches" of sound—a layer of dialogue, two layers of traffic, a layer of automobile horns, of seagulls, of crowd hubbub, of footsteps, waves hitting the beach, foghorns, outboard motors, distant thunder, fireworks, and on and on. All playing together at the same time. (For the purposes of this discussion, let's define a *layer* as a conceptually-unified series of sounds which run more or less continuously, without any large gaps between individual sounds. A single seagull cry, for instance, does not make a layer.)

The problem, of course, is that sooner or later (mostly sooner) this kind of intense layering winds up sounding like the rush of sound between radio stations—*white noise*—which is where we began our discussion. The trouble with white *noise* is that, like white *light*, there is not a lot of information to be extracted from it. Or rather there is so much information tangled together that it is impossible for the mind to separate it back out. It is as indigestible as one of Dagwood's sandwiches. You still *hear* everything, technically speaking, but it is impossible to *listen* to it, to appreciate or even truly distinguish any single element. So the filmmakers would have done all that work, put all those sounds together, for nothing. They could have just tuned between radio stations and gotten the same result.

This short section of *Apocalypse Now* is a good illustration of what we've been talking about. Colonel Kilgore (Robert Duvall) has staged an attack on "Charlie's Point" because it has the best surfing waves in Vietnam. His helicopters are landing on the beach, with "The Ride of the Valkyries" blasting from loudspeakers amid gunfire and explosions. One of the American soldiers is severely wounded by a secondary explosion and the Medics move in to help evacuate him. This minute of film is part of a much longer action sequence of equal intensity.

Originally, back in 1978, we organized the sound this way because we didn't have enough playback machines—we *couldn't* run everything together: there were over a hundred and seventy-five separate soundtracks for this section of film alone. It was my very own Dagwood sandwich. So I had to break the sound down into smaller, more manageable groups, called *premixes*, of about thirty tracks each. But I still do the same thing today, even though I may have three times as many faders as I did back then.

The six premix layers were:

1. Dialogue
2. Helicopters
3. Music ("The Valkyries")
4. Small arms fire (AK-47s and M-16s)
5. Explosions (Mortars, Grenades, Heavy Artillery)
6. Footsteps and other Foley-type sounds.

These layers are listed in order of importance, in somewhat the same way that you might arrange the instrumental groups in an orchestra. Mural painters do a similar thing when they grid a wall into squares and just deal with one square at a time. What murals and mixing and music all have in common is that in each of them the detail has to be so exactly proportioned to the immense scale of the work that it is easy to go wrong—either the details will overwhelm the eye (or ear) but give no sense of the whole, or the whole will be complete but without convincing details.

The human voice must be understood clearly in almost all circumstances, whether it is singing in an opera or dialogue in a film, so the first thing I did was mix the dialogue for this scene, isolated from any competing elements.

Then I asked myself: what is the next most dominant sound in the scene? In this case it happened to be the helicopters, so I mixed all the helicopter tracks together onto a separate roll of 35mm film, while listening to the playback of the dialogue, to make sure I didn't do anything with the helicopters to obscure the dialogue.

Then I progressed to the third most dominant sound, which was "The Ride of the Valkyries" as played through the amplifiers of Kilgore's helicopters. I mixed this to a third roll of film while monitoring the two previous premixes of helicopters and dialogue.

And so on, from #4 (small arms fire) through #5 (explosions) to #6 (footsteps). In the end, I had six premixes of film, each one a six-channel master (three channels behind the screen: left, centre, and right; two channels in the back of the theatre: left and right; and one channel for low frequency enhancement). Each premix was balanced against the others so that—theoretically, anyway—the final mix should simply have been a question of playing everything together at one set level.

What I found, to my dismay, however, was that in the first rehearsal of the final mix everything seemed to collapse into that big ball of noise I was talking about earlier. Each of the sound-groups I had premixed was justified by what was happening on screen, but by some devilish alchemy they all melted into an unimpressive racket when they were played together.

The challenge seemed to be to somehow find a balance point where there were enough interesting sounds to add meaning and help tell the story, but not so many that they overwhelmed each other.

The question was: where was that balance point?

Suddenly I remembered my experience ten years earlier with Robot Footsteps, and my first encounter with the mysterious Law of Two-and-a-Half.

Robots and Grapes

THIS HAD HAPPENED in 1969, on one of the first films I worked on: George Lucas's *THX-1138*. It was a low-budget film, but it was also science fiction, so my job was to produce an otherworldly soundtrack on a shoestring. The shoestring part was easy, because that was the only way I had worked up till then. The otherworldly part, though, meant that most of the sounds that automatically "came with" the image (the sync sound) had to be replaced. A case in point: the footsteps of the policemen in the film, who were supposed to be robots made out of six hundred pounds of steel and chrome. During filming, of course, these robots were actors in costume who made the normal sound that anyone would make when they walked. But in the film we wanted them to sound massive, so I built some special metal shoes, fitted with springs and iron plates, and went to the Museum of Natural History in San Francisco at 2 a.m., put them on and recorded lots of separate "walk-bys" in different sonic environments, stalking around like some kind of Frankenstein's monster.

They sounded great, but I now had to sync all these footsteps up. We would do this differently today—the footsteps would be recorded on what is called a Foley stage, in sync with the picture right from the beginning. But I was young and idealistic—I wanted it to sound right!—and besides, we didn't have the money to go to Los Angeles and rent a Foley stage.

So there I was with my overflowing basket of footsteps, laying them in the film one at a time, like doing embroidery or something. It was going well, but too slowly, and I was afraid I wouldn't finish in time for the mix. Luckily, one morning at 2 a.m. a good fairy came to my rescue in the form of a sudden and accidental realization: that if there was one robot, his footsteps had to be in sync; if there were two robots, also, their footsteps had to be in sync; but if there were three robots, nothing had to be in sync. Or rather, any sync point was as good as any other!

This discovery broke the logjam, and I was able to finish in time for the mix. But . . .

But why does something like this happen?

Somehow, it seems that our minds can keep track of one person's footsteps, or even the footsteps of two people, but with three or more people our minds just give up—there are too many steps happening too quickly. As a result, each footstep is no longer evaluated individually, but rather the *group of footsteps* is evaluated as a single entity, like a musical chord. If the pace of the steps is roughly correct, and it seems as if they are on the right surface, this is apparently enough. In effect, the mind says "Yes, I see *a group* of people walking down a

corridor and what I hear sounds like *a group* of people walking down a corridor."

Sometime during the mid-nineteenth century, one of Edouard Manet's students was painting a bunch of grapes, diligently outlining every single one, and Manet suddenly knocked the brush out of her hand and shouted: "Not like that! I don't give a damn about Every Single Grape! I want you to get the feel of the grapes, how they taste, their colour, how the dust shapes them and softens them at the same time."

Similarly, if you have gotten Every Single Footstep in sync but failed to capture the energy of the group, the space through which they are moving, the surface on which they are walking, and so on, you have made the same kind of mistake that Manet's student was making. You have paid too much attention to something that the mind is incapable of assimilating anyway, even if it wanted to.

Trees and Forests

AT ANY RATE, after my robot experience I became sensitive to the transformation that appears to happen as soon as you have three of anything. On a practical level, it saved me a lot of work—I found many places where I didn't have to count the grapes, so to speak—but I began to see the same pattern occurring in other areas as well, and it had implications far beyond footsteps.

The clearest example of what I mean can be seen in the Chinese symbols for "tree" and "forest." In Chinese, the word "tree" actually looks like a tree—sort of a pine tree with drooping limbs. And the Chinese word for "forest" is three trees. Now, it was obviously up to the Chinese how many trees were needed to convey the idea of "forest," but two didn't seem to be enough, I guess, and sixteen, say, was way too many—it would have taken too long to write and would have just messed up the page. But three trees seems to be just right. So in evolving their writing system, the ancient Chinese came across the same fact that I blundered into with my robot footsteps: that three is the borderline where you cross over from "individual things" to "group."

It turns out Bach also had some things to say about this phenomenon in music, relative to the maximum number of melodic lines a listener can appreciate simultaneously, which he believed was three. And I think it is the reason that Barnum's circuses have three rings, not five, or two. Even in religion you can detect its influence when you compare Zoroastrian Duality to the mysterious "multiple singularity" of the Christian Trinity. And the counting systems of many primitive tribes (and some animals) end at three, beyond which more is simply "many."

So what began to interest me from a creative point of view was the point where I could see the forest *and* the trees—where there was simultaneously Clarity, which comes through a feeling for the individual elements (the notes), and Density, which comes through a feeling for the whole (the chord). And I found this balance point to occur most often when there were *not quite* three layers of something. I came to nickname this my "Law of Two-and-a-Half."

Left and Right

NOW, A PRACTICAL RESULT of our earlier distinction between Encoded sound and Embodied sound seems to be that this Law of Two-and-a-Half applies only to sounds of the same "colour"—sounds *from the same part of the conceptual spectrum.* (With sounds from *different parts* of the spectrum—different coloured sounds—there seems to be more leeway.)

The robot footsteps, for instance, were all the same "green," so by the time there were three layers, they had congealed into a new singularity: *robots walking in a group.* Similarly, it is just possible to follow two "violet" conversations simultaneously, but not three. Listen again to the scene in *The Godfather* where the family is sitting around wondering what to do if the Godfather (Marlon Brando) dies. Sonny is talking to Tom, and Clemenza is talking to Tessio—you can follow both conversa-

Mark Berger, Francis Ford Coppola, and Walter Murch mixing
The Godfather Part II

tions and also pay attention to Michael making a phone call to Luca Brasi (Michael on the phone is the "half" of the two-and-a-half), but only because the scene was carefully written and performed and recorded. Or think about two pieces of "red" music playing simultaneously: a background radio and a thematic score. It can be pulled off, but it has to be done carefully.

But if you blend sounds from different parts of the spectrum, you get some extra latitude. Dialogue and music can live together quite happily. Add some sound effects, too, and everything still sounds transparent: two people talking, with an accompanying musical score, and some birds in the background, maybe some traffic. Very nice, even though we already have four layers.

Why is this? Well, it probably has something to do with the areas of the brain in which this information is processed. It appears that Encoded sound (language) is dealt with mostly on the left side of the brain, and Embodied sound (music) is taken care of across the hall, on the right. There are exceptions, of course: for instance, it appears that the rhythmic elements of music are dealt with on the left, and the vowels of speech on the right. But generally speaking, the two departments seem to be able to operate simultaneously without getting in each other's way. What this means is that by dividing up the work they can deal with a total number of layers that would be impossible for either side individually.

Density and Clarity

In fact, it seems that the total number of layers, if the burden is evenly spread across the spectrum from Encoded to Embodied (from "violet" dialogue to "red" music) is *double* what it would be if the layers were stacked up in any one region (colour) of the spectrum. In other words, you can manage five layers instead of two-and-a-half, thanks to the left-right duality of the human brain. What this might mean, in practical terms, is:

1. One layer of "violet" dialogue;
2. One layer of "red" music;
3. One layer of "cool" (linguistic) effects (e.g., footsteps);
4. One layer of "warm" (musical) effects (e.g., atmospheric tonalities);
5. One layer of "yellow" (equally balanced "centaur") effects.

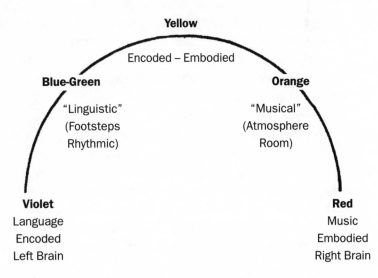

WHAT I AM SUGGESTING is that, at any one moment (for practical purposes, let's say that a "moment" is any five-second section of film), five layers is the maximum that can be tolerated by an audience if you also want them to maintain a clear sense of the individual elements that are contributing to the mix. In other words, if you want the experience to be simultaneously Dense and Clear.

But the precondition for being able to sustain five layers is that the layers be spread evenly across the conceptual spectrum. If the sounds stack up in one region (one colour), the limit shrinks to two-and-a-half. If you want to have two-and-a-half layers of dialogue, for instance, and you want people to understand every word, you had better eliminate the competition from any other sounds that might be running at the same time.

To highlight the differences in our perception of Encoded vs. Embodied sound, it is interesting to note the paradox that in almost all stereo films produced over the last twenty-five years the dialogue is always placed in the centre, no matter what the actual position is of the actors on the screen: they could be on the far left, but their voices still come out of the centre. And yet everyone (including us mixers) still believes the voices are "coming from" the actors. This is a completely different treatment than is given sound effects of the "yellow" variety—car pass-bys, for instance— which are routinely (and almost obligatorily) moved around the screen with the action. And certainly different from "red" music, which is usually arranged so that it comes out of all speakers in the

theatre (including the surrounds) simultaneously. Embodied "orange" sound effects (atmospheres, room tones) are also given a full stereo treatment. "Blue-green" sound effects like footsteps, however, are usually placed in the centre like dialogue, unless the filmmakers want to call special attention to the steps, and then they will be placed and moved along with the action. But in this case the actors almost always have no dialogue.

As a general rule, then, the "warmer" the sound, the more it tends to be given a full stereo (multi-track) treatment, whereas the "cooler" the sound, the more it tends to be monophonically placed in the centre. And yet we seem to have no problem with this incongruity—just the opposite, in fact. The early experiments (in the 1950s) which involved moving the dialogue around the screen were eventually abandoned as seeming "artificial."

Monophonic films have always been this way— that part is not new. What is new and peculiar, though, is that we are able to tolerate, even enjoy, the mixture of mono and stereo in the same film.

Why is this? I believe it has something to do with the way we decode language, and that when our brains are busy with Encoded sound, we willingly abandon any question of its origin to the visual, allowing the image to "steer" the source of the sound. When the sound is Embodied, however, and little linguistic decoding is going on, the location of the sound in space becomes more and more important the less linguistic it is. In the terms of this lecture, the "warmer" it is. The fact that we can process both Encoded mono and Embodied stereo simultaneously seems to clearly demonstrate some of the differences in the way our two hemispheres operate.

Getting back to my problem on *Apocalypse*: it appeared to be caused by having six layers of sound, and six layers is essentially the same as sixteen, or sixty: I had passed a threshold beyond which the sounds congeal into a new singularity—dense noise in which a fragment or two can perhaps be distinguished, but not the developmental lines of the layers themselves. With six layers, I had achieved *Density*, but at the expense of *Clarity*.

What I did as a result was to restrict the layers for that section of film to a maximum of five. By luck or by design, I could do this, because my sounds were spread evenly across the conceptual spectrum.

1. Dialogue (violet)
2. Small arms fire (blue-green "words" that say "Shot! Shot! Shot!")
3. Explosions (yellow "kettle drums" with content)
4. Footsteps and miscellaneous (blue to orange)
5. Helicopters (orange music-like drones)
6. "Valkyries" Music (red)

If the layers had not been as evenly spread out, the limit would have been less than five. And as I mentioned before, if they had all been concentrated in one "colour zone" of the spectrum (all violet or all red, for instance), the limit would have shrunk to two-and-a-half. It seems, then, that the more monochrome the palette, the fewer the layers that can be super-imposed; the more polychrome the palette, on the other hand, the more layers you get to play with.

So in this section of *Apocalypse*, I found I could build a "sandwich" with five layers to it. If I wanted to add something new, I had to take something else away. For instance, when the boy in the helicopter says "I'm not going, I'm not going!" I chose to remove all the music. On a certain logical level, that is not reasonable, because he is actually *in* the helicopter that is producing the music, so it should be louder there than anywhere else. But for story reasons we needed to hear his dialogue, of course, and I also wanted to emphasize the chaos outside—the AK-47s and mortar fire that he was resisting going into—and the helicopter sound that represented "safety," as well as the voices of the other members of his unit. So for that brief section, here are the layers:

1. Dialogue ("I'm not going! I'm not going!")
2. Other voices, shouts, etc.
3. Helicopters
4. AK-47s and M-16s
5. Mortar fire

Under the circumstances, music was the sacrificial victim. The miraculous thing is that you do not hear it go away—you believe that it is still playing, even though, as I mentioned earlier, it should be louder here than anywhere else. And, in fact, as soon as this line of dialogue was over, we brought the music back in and sacrificed something else. Every moment in this section is similarly fluid, a kind of shell game where layers are disappearing and reappearing according to the dramatic focus of the moment. It is necessitated by the "five-layer" law, but it is also one of the things that makes the soundtrack exciting to listen to.

But I should emphasize that this does not mean I *always* had five layers cooking. Conceptual density is something that should obey the same rules as loudness dynamics. Your mix, moment by moment, should be as dense (or as loud) as the story and events warrant. A monotonously dense soundtrack is just as wearing as a monotonously loud film. Just as a symphony would be unendurable if all the instruments played together all the time. But my point is that, under the most favourable of circumstances, five layers is a threshold which should not be surpassed thoughtlessly, just as you should not thoughtlessly surpass loud-ness thresholds. Both thresholds seem to have some basis in our neurobiology.

The bottom line is that the audience is primarily involved in following the story: despite everything I have said, the right thing to do is ultimately whatever serves the storytelling, in the widest sense. When this helicopter landing scene is over, however, my hope was to leave a lasting impression of everything happening at once—Density—yet everything heard distinctly—Clarity. In fact, as you can see, simultaneous Density and Clarity can only be achieved by a kind of subterfuge.

As I said at the beginning, it can be complicated to be simple and simple to be complicated.

But sometimes it is just complicated to be complicated.

. . . One day just before the shooting [on Rashomon] *was to start, the three assistant directors Daiei had assigned me came to see me at the inn where I was staying. I wondered what the problem could be. It turned out that they found the script baffling and wanted me to explain it to them. "Please read it again more carefully," I told them. "If you read it diligently, you should be able to understand it because it was written with the intention of being comprehensible." But they wouldn't leave. "We believe we have read it carefully, and we still don't understand it at all; that's why we want you to explain it to us." For their persistence I gave them this simple explanation:*

"Human beings are unable to be honest with themselves about themselves. They cannot talk about themselves without embellishing. This script portrays such human beings—the kind who cannot survive without lies to make them feel they are better people than they really are. It even shows this sinful need for flattering falsehood going beyond the grave—even the character who dies cannot give up his lies when he speaks to the living through a medium. Egoism is a sin the human being carries with him from birth; it is the most difficult to redeem. This film is like a strange picture scroll that is unrolled and displayed by the ego. You say that you can't understand this script at all, but that is because the human heart itself is impossible to understand. If you focus on the impossibility of truly understanding human psychology and read the script one more time, I think you will grasp the point of it."

After I finished, two of the three assistant directors nodded and said they would try reading the script again. They got up to leave, but the third, who was the chief, remained unconvinced. He left with an angry look on his face. (As it turned out, this chief assistant director and I never did get along. I still regret that in the end I had to ask for his resignation. But, aside from this, the work went well.)

— AKIRA KUROSAWA, *Notes on Filmmaking*

Que Viva Mexico!

The Folly of Upton Sinclair and Sergei Eisenstein

JEFF BIGGERS

We heard the roar from the truck's loudspeakers long before the vehicle came into sight. Dropping into the canyon village on a road carved along the creek bed, the truck blasted norteño tunes off the bluffs as if rallying a valley of polka dancers.

The dirt road into the Tarahumara village in the Sierra Madre where we lived for a year, never had much traffic. Logging trucks descended from the high plateaus, occasional tourist vans arrived from Creel, Coca-Cola and packaged food vendors made their deliveries to the village co-op shop with the fanfare of Pony Express runners, and on Sundays, two vegetable trucks would converge on the village gathering, blaring out norteño on competing sound systems.

We watched this new truck jostle into view from the side of our neighbour's house. It looked like an old furniture-moving van. I was finishing laying the beams for the roof of a chicken coop with my neighbor Pedro and another villager, Ruben.

"Machine guns, violence, *The Revenge of the Tarahumara*!" the loudspeaker continued to blast.

"It's movie night," Pedro said, smiling.

The cinema was assembled on the side of the old mission walls. A carnival tent rose, with a screen on one end. Rickety chairs were scattered in rows on the ground.

I was curious to see the turnout. So few people lived within listening distance of the loudspeakers, even if the noise echoed far into the canyons with relentless tunes and announcements. The tent was packed when I arrived. Over fifty people wobbled in their seats, wearing sombreros, caps or scarves. Kids had escaped from the boarding school and straddled the towering mission walls for a peek. A reel-to-reel projector snapped the images in the picture from the side of the truck, which roared with the only generator in the area. *The Revenge of the Tarahumara* was actually about a Yaqui in Sonora, played by an Italian-looking actor, who rescues his kidnapped son from the evil Mexican grandfather. His Yaqui sister was played by an actress who resembled Jane Russell in deer hides. In the end, the father takes a few bullets, but survives, and everyone, including the blond son, is happy. The crowd cheered at the bloody end.

The next movies revolved around the narco-traficantes. There was one basic plot: one cartel fought another for control of the drug market, with enough machine guns, hard drinking, big-breasted women and polyester suits to shame Scarface into retirement.

The Mexican film industry dated back to a series of short films, made and introduced by Frenchman Gabriel Veyre in 1896. It had always been obsessed with violence and indigenous populations. Those first films included *A Pistol Duel in the Woods at Chapultepec*, *The Breakfast of Indians*, and *The Cockfight*. Over the next decades, the Mexican industry produced scores of adventure and romantic films, including those by Guillermo "El Indio" Calles, a man who claimed to be of indigenous origins from Chihuahua. Calles acted and directed in over sixty films with a distinct indigenous bent, including *The Yaqui Indian*, *The Aztec Race*, and *The Bronze Race*. I had seen him once in an American movie, a box office adventure hit in 1956, *Run for the Sun*, about an American journalist's airplane crash in the Mexican jungles, in search of Nazi fugitives.

A week after *The Revenge of the Yaqui-cum-Tarahumara*, the novelist Alfredo Vea and his wife Carole Conn arrived for a visit. They had taken the train from the Los Mochis coastal area, on the other side of the Sierra Madre, not far from the Rio Yaqui, the homeland of Alfredo's grandfather. We told them about the films; some of the villagers eyed Alfredo as if he might have been one of those wily narcos in the movies.

The best film about indigenous cultures and violence in Mexico would never be screened in this Tarahumara village. It was never fully screened anywhere in the world. Sergei Eisenstein's *Que Viva Mexico!*, in fact, nearly vanished in international scandal.

I first learned the details of Eisenstein's folly in the letters of Upton Sinclair, when Alfredo and I, on a typical 102-degree day in the Sonoran Desert, had gone in search of Sinclair's unknown home in Buckeye, Arizona. In one of the best kept secrets in the Western states, Sinclair lived in anonymity in this boarded-up desert town with his ailing wife, coolly sitting out the McCarthy years. Sinclair wrote over eighty books; he would complete his autobiography down the street from the high school. From this desert hamlet, Sinclair also maintained a relentless correspondence with some of the great minds of the world, chronicling his own life story, as if obsessed with ensuring his immortality in the history books. It didn't work in Buckeye; the town acted as if "the communist sympathizer," in the words of one teacher, had never resided there.

Sinclair's house was unmistakable, ringed by an imposing seven-foot-high brick wall. It was a small bungalow on the corner of a low-income residential street. It was a long way from Sinclair's New York City highrise or the southern California villa where he entertained Sergei Eisenstein in 1930. The deed was in the name of Hunter Kimbrough, who had been the inept manager of Eisenstein's film.

We entered a yard strewn with beer cans and spare auto parts. A cage of fowl sat in the corner. We knocked on a front door that was cracked, a torn and discoloured sheet in the front window. We had no luck in stirring the ghosts.

As we drove out of town, Alfredo noted the signs of better times when Buckeye Road wasn't overlooked or considered the transit zone between two dead ends.

"It's almost as if Upton Sinclair wanted to lose himself out here," he said.

His Yaqui grandfather had forewarned his grandson of such a displacement of the soul. Vea had recorded in his first novel, *La Maravilla*:

To lose yourself is the greatest mutilation . . . Mexico is an old word, mijo. It means the navel of the moon . . . to the gringo immortality means from today forward, mijo; each gringo wants to live forever. That's what they want from their God, that's what they want from their medicine. To a Yaqui immortality can also mean from today backward to the beginning. The future is no longer than the past. They are the same distance no matter where you stand.

Given the tragicomic making of *Que Viva Mexico!*, Sergei Eisenstein, unlike Upton Sinclair, would have understood Alfredo's grandfather.

THE COUPLING of Upton Sinclair and Sergei Eisenstein, two of the world's most widely recognized writers and directors in 1930—introduced, no less, by the wily Charlie Chaplin—heralded the making of the "greatest film ever." Conceived as a paean to the rebirth of indigenous cultures and the revolution in Mexico, *Que Viva Mexico!* turned out to be the silent film industry's most calamitous miscarriage. In the process, the tragicomedy of errors behind the making of the film nearly destroyed the careers of both men.

First lured to Hollywood to make pictures for Paramount, Sergei Eisenstein had become world-renowned in the 1920s for his film direction genius in the Russian masterpieces *Strike* and *The Battleship Potemkin*. His ground-breaking film editing "montage" techniques—cross-cutting between images to heighten emotions—remain a lasting influence in cinema today.

Born in Riga, Latvia, in 1898, two years after Gabriel Veyre had brought the moving pictures to Mexico, Eisenstein's obsession with that country was born in the theatre. In 1921, he designed the scenery and costumes for the Moscow production of *The Mexican*, a play based on the short story by Jack London. With a carnivalesque drama, the play chronicled the boxing feats of a young man at the time of the revolution. A few years later, Eisenstein met the celebrated painter and muralist Diego Rivera, propelling "a burning desire to travel" to Mexico. Rivera turned Eisenstein onto Anita Brenner's critical work, *Idols Behind Altars*, which detailed an obsession shared by Eisenstein with the mockery and rituals of death in Mexican art and culture, and focussed the director's attention on the acts of indigenous people who hid their native idols behind the cloak of Catholic altars.

After making a lecture tour through Europe, including pit-stops in Berlin, Paris, Zurich and London, Eisenstein arrived in Hollywood in the spring of 1930 and signed a contract with Paramount films. He had the permission of the Soviet film division. Sound films had already begun to make waves in the American market, led by a commercial competition unknown in the Soviet Union. Despite Eisenstein's fame and prestige among the Hollywood denizens, including a close friendship with Charlie Chaplin, the Russian director's more oblique film concepts never suited the commercial expectations of the American producers; numerous ideas and scripts were either rejected or fell through, including Eisenstein's scenario for a film based on Theodore Dreiser's *An American Tragedy*. In October, 1930, Paramount publicly terminated Eisenstein's contract.

So close to the Mexican border, Eisenstein refused to allow the Paramount debacle to force his premature return to the Soviet Union. Prompted by Chaplin, he contacted Upton Sinclair, who had long been a Socialist supporter of the Soviet Union. Living then in Pasadena, Sinclair had become one of the most widely translated American authors; in that same year, over 525 titles of his work had appeared in 34 countries. Nearly two million copies of his books had been distributed in the Soviet Union. In his Nobel Prize nomination of Sinclair in 1932, co-signed by Bertrand Russell, Albert Einstein, John Dewey and numerous others, George Bernard Shaw championed Sinclair's unique literary role in altering history rather than any stylistic triumph.

Always one to take up a good cause, Sinclair and his wife, neither of whom had ever dealt with the financial aspects of filmmaking (Sinclair had sold a couple of his books for film production), agreed to serve as the producers and fundraisers of the film in Mexico. They summoned Sinclair's brother-in-law Hunter Kimbrough, a Southern gentleman and one-time stock salesman, to serve as the on-site general manager of the film in Mexico. Kimbrough maintained a self-professed "dislike for artists." As a sign of things to come,

teetotaller Sinclair begged Kimbrough on the day of departure to "promise not to drink" in Mexico.

Having thrown out a casual figure of $25,000, Eisenstein and the Sinclairs agreed to a contract that would have "no strings attached," with the expectation that the film would take three to four months to shoot. Eisenstein, naturally, would return to Hollywood to edit the film. In this mood of enthusiasm and camaraderie, Sinclair raised the figure to $50,000 before Eisenstein and his party of two assistants and Kimbrough arrived in Mexico in December 1930.

Sinclair couldn't resist sending his own ideas for the film. In a letter to Eisenstein, he proposed the story of a young man, "raised on Indian superstitions," who leaves the mountains for a trip to see the world and comes in contact with modern science and ideas, only to reject them and return to his native home, "a sadder and still more uncertain man." According to Sinclair, "to portray an Indian boy coming into contact with the new currents in Mexico and shrinking back from them bewildered, will be about as safe a theme as you can choose."

Eisenstein had no plans, other than naming the film *Da zdravstvuyet Meksika!* His reception in Mexico City was nothing less than "royal." His photo graced the front pages of the Mexican newspapers. He soon remade contact with Diego Rivera and other Mexican artists, as well as the American writer Katherine Anne Porter. Within the first days, he began filming the Fiesta of the Virgin of Guadalupe, as well as a local bullfight.

Two weeks later, Eisenstein and his party were arrested by the Mexican police under the false charges of seeking to disseminate Bolshevik propaganda. The whole affair ended up a blunder for the Mexican government, which issued an apology to Sinclair, by the Secretary of Foreign Relations, within a few days.

Meanwhile, Sinclair was not only having problems raising money in an economy that was still feeling the tremors of the Stock Market Crash, but was facing the objections of the head of the Russian film division in the States; the Soviets cringed at the depiction of Eisenstein as an artist freed from the control of the state apparatus.

After a month of "listening to the heartbeat of Mexico," Eisenstein still possessed no storyline. An earthquake in Oaxaca, however, on January 14th, propelled the crew in that direction. Eisenstein managed to shoot over 1,200 feet of film, making headlines in the States. The film party eagerly believed they would be able to sell the film to United Press or other media outlets. The actual film, however, while the first on the scene, was delayed in a maze of Mexican censor offices, crushing hopes of any deals. In the meantime, Eisenstein was summoned once again by the authorities, though this time by mistake; the chief of the central police department of Mexico had confused Eisenstein

with Albert Einstein, and immediately released the party from any engagements.

In an effort to raise funds, Sinclair then developed and showed the first footage or rushes of Mexico taken by Eisenstein to a select group of observers, including Albert Einstein. This act, while in his interest, outraged Eisenstein, who had yet to view the material, and he demanded that Sinclair agree never to do any previews again.

The filming then progressed, taking Eisenstein and his party to Tehuantepec and the Yucatan, and parts throughout Mexico. For Sinclair, however, the fundraising and financial details had become an albatross around his writing career, forcing the cancellation of lecture trips to Europe and even the Soviet Union. With Eisenstein's permission, Sinclair then showed more of the footage, which had been sent in instalments with great difficulty (due to customs and censors) to the Mexican Vice Consul, who declared "these pictures will be a revelation even to the Mexicans."

The Soviets' fears intensified. Wary of Eisenstein veering from proscribed policies on film topics, themes and styles, they demanded that Eisenstein clarify his scenario in writing and submit it to their own film division. Instead, owing to illness and the rainy season, Eisenstein wrote to Sinclair that he would not be able finish the film for $50,000. The Sinclairs, at their wit's end on raising funds—Mary Sinclair had mortgaged some of her properties—suddenly realized their once-informal agreement had unravelled. In a moment of panic, they even sought to sell the rights to the entire project. Sinclair also approached officials in the Soviet Union with a deal that would exchange the royalties on his books for $25,000 to be invested directly in the movie. Meanwhile, a growing and fierce anti-Bolshevik movement, led by Major Frank Peace, started to make some inroads with the press about revoking Eisenstein's visa status in the United States.

At this point, tempers were unleashed in a teeming exchange of letters and telegraphs between Sinclair, Eisenstein and the rest of the party in Mexico. In need of film, Eisenstein obstinately declared that he could not finish the project for $50,000; desperate to raise funds, Sinclair repeatedly cabled to Eisenstein to adhere to his earlier word. Despite a modest investment of 5,000 rubles by the Soviet Union, the fundraising fell from dismal to an outright crisis.

In July, the film party made headlines again when one of the actors, a boy who played a bandit, took a loaded pistol and accidentally shot and killed his sister. (Ever the creative genius, Sinclair would later pitch the story as a film promo for a leading magazine.)

Finally, in August, Eisenstein sent a complete outline of *Que Viva Mexico!*, via Kimbrough, breaking the film into six parts. However, Sinclair, on the verge of a nervous breakdown and suffering from delaying a hernia operation, dismissed the outline and beseeched Eisenstein to modify the film to meet the original budget. Outraged by the suggestion, resisting any hint of compromise, Eisenstein saw his relationship with Sinclair and Kimbrough transform from bad to worse. According to Kimbrough's letters to Sinclair, "I am little rough on him (Eisenstein) these days . . . He's like a Negro. Kind words and considerations are not enough."

At one of the worst ebbs in the correspondence, however, the Soviet film division suddenly announced their interest in following up on Sinclair's proposal to invest $25,000 in the film. The investment was hardly without strings, and included a clause for a partnership in the control of the film. In September, in the midst of negotiations, both Sinclair and his wife were rushed to the hospital—Mary Sinclair for ptomaine poisoning, while Sinclair collapsed due to exhaustion and a kidney infection. While the filming proceeded, Sinclair was then notified of the arrival of a M.G.M. film unit in Mexico to make a rival film.

Despite the relatively positive negotiations with the Soviets, Sinclair could barely withstand the pressure caused by the film, and began to express a bitter resentment at Eisenstein's lack of correspondence to match his daily notes. In October, he attempted to give the film director a glimpse of reality by noting that "Germany is likely to declare herself bankrupt any day . . . and if that happens, it means quite certainly that the Bank of England will have to close." He added, "in the three days when Wall Street financiers were commuting between New York City and the White House, there was serious doubt whether anything could be saved from the wreckage." Sinclair concluded: "This is the situation upon which you propose to go on spending money without limit."

Unaware of the internal politics in the Soviet Union and their film bureau, Sinclair continued the investment negotiations in a concrete fashion.

PHOTO BY

G. ALEXANDROV

S. M. EISENSTEIN

COLLECTIVE

PRODUCTIONS

By November, however, one of Eisenstein's archrivals and enemies in the film division took control and dismissed the Soviet negotiator in the States. In a foreshadowing of the purges to come, the Stalinist forces launched a chain of events to discredit Eisenstein's name and ideas.

Still overwhelmed by the beauty of Mexico and shooting stunning footage on track with his six-part plan, Eisenstein's ventures were halted again by the Mexican censors in the Los Angeles consulate, who insisted on reviewing the new footage before it was handed over to Sinclair. The consul objected to scenes depicting horses, ridden by ruthless landlords and their hired guns, trampling the heads of half-buried peasant boys. These tremors of controversy were nothing compared to a chilling cable sent directly to Sinclair by Joseph Stalin himself: "Eisenstein loose [sic] his comrades confidence in Soviet Union . . . he is thought to be deserter who broke off with his own country."

Sinclair responded with a long and detailed defense of Eisenstein, addressing the letter to Comrade Stalin. Fearful of alerting Eisenstein of the cable, and risking an emotional tailspin, Sinclair continued to exchange letters in search of a conclusion to the film, to which Eisenstein only responded that the film would be an "absolute flop" unless he received more money.

At this point, Sinclair received notice that the Soviet Union was planning to withdraw any investment. It considered Eisenstein's intention to remain in Mexico a breach of faith. (Whether or not Eisenstein publicly expressed his desire to stay away from the Soviet Union, he did inquire about various film projects in India, Japan, and other foreign locations.) When Kimbrough arrived in Pasadena, having completely broken off his relationship with Eisenstein, he forced Sinclair to grant him complete authority over the film direction in Mexico. A beleaguered Sinclair agreed.

By the end of 1931, the exchanges between Sinclair, Eisenstein and Kimbrough were reduced to accusations and counter-accusations. At odds over the accounting of the budget, both Eisenstein and Kimbrough referred unabashedly to each other as liars. (Kimbrough accused Eisenstein of hiring an assassin; Eisenstein claimed Kimbrough was a drunk, who had even been tossed in a Mexican jail for a raucous episode with prostitutes; Kimbrough countered that Eisenstein was "some kind of a pervert" and a homosexual.) The Sinclairs, meanwhile, "argued for days and nights," according to Sinclair; Mary Sinclair demanded an immediate termination of the filming. While Sinclair attempted to salvage the Soviet connection, as well as other investors, he plunged over $20,000 from the film rights of his own novel, *Wet Parade*, into Eisenstein's project, relieving his wife of any financial responsibilities. Embroiled in the details of the film, Sinclair's own writing career had been completely put aside for the entire year.

In January 1932, rejected by the Soviet Union, which had reneged on its promise to invest, and with his own life in shambles, Sinclair wired to Kimbrough to "permit no further shooting . . . come home immediately . . . bring party." Stunned by the news, all members of the party, including Kimbrough, attempted to make up their differences and continued shooting until the end of the month. Eisenstein even insisted on finishing the final segment of the film. In a disingenuous attempt to stay in the country and finish his project—and thus, return to the Soviet Union with a great achievement that justified the over-extended leave—Eisenstein cabled the Soviet authorities that he was bound by his contract and government restrictions to remain in Mexico.

Feeling betrayed by Eisenstein's delaying tactics, Sinclair advised the director that he took no responsibility in his relationship with Moscow. He repeatedly demanded that the party return at once. Once their film was exhausted (Eisenstein shot over 200,000 feet), Kimbrough and Eisenstein finally capitulated. On February 17th, having driven from Mexico City, the party arrived at the Texas border, only to be detained by customs officials. Eisenstein and his Russian assistants were held for several days, until Sinclair could convince several senators to issue a short-term visa. Given the delay, Sinclair agreed that Eisenstein should return to Moscow and cut the film, instead of returning to Hollywood. Unveiling his incorrigible optimism to the press, Sinclair declared publicly that the film would be a smashing success on the screen in three to four months. Eisenstein was finally released and drove to New York, with the intention of catching a ship to Europe.

DESPITE HIS LETTERS OF INTENT to ship the film to Moscow for Eisenstein's editing, Sinclair went into a final tailspin of his own in the spring of 1932. Instead of heading home directly, Eisenstein lingered in New York, outraging the Soviet officials and Sinclair and his investors, while releasing conflicting statements concerning his plans. Meanwhile, Sinclair was also shown numerous boxes of "obscene" drawings by Eisenstein, taken from his personal belongings, which depicted sexual acts between various religious figures, including Jesus on the cross. Eisenstein also attempted to charge Sinclair for the cost of his travel back to the Soviet Union, for which he had already been given $4,000 by Paramount.

Sinclair snapped. Writing a lengthy letter about his relationship with Eisenstein, addressed to the Soviet authorities and even Comrade Stalin, Sinclair detailed his numerous crises and controversies with the film director. In a total shift of his position, Sinclair then brazenly declared his intention to keep the film in the States and allow another editor to carry out the final cut. The disclosure incensed Eisenstein, the Soviet authorities, virtually every director of note in Hollywood, and the Communist Left in the States, which had been following the entire filming process in the press. With only his notebooks and drawings, Eisenstein finally boarded a ship for Europe.

On May 10, 1933, the world premiere of *Thunder Over Mexico* took place in Los Angeles at the Carthay Circle Theatre. The production of the film had been handed over to Sol Lesser, then with Principal Pictures, who would later go on to fame and fortune by producing the *Tarzan* films; he won an Academy Award in 1951 for *Kon Tiki*. Sinclair, who had been bitterly assailed over the year by both leftists and artists as a sell-out, a betrayer and a white-boned devil for refusing to allow Eisenstein to complete the movie, appeared briefly on the stage after the screening. He declared, "the man who directed this film is rated by many as the greatest director of our time." At another showing in New York, Sinclair was provided with a police escort. The New York Herald declared Que Viva Mexico!, "is the most controversial film in the world." According to one critic, without Eisenstein's editing touch, the film was "pretty dull stuff."

The actual film was only a fragment—the dramatic story of a peon who is abused and then brutally murdered by the pre-revolution feudal lords—of the planned six stories by Eisenstein. Lesser eventually carved nearly 200,000 feet of film into *Thunder Over Mexico* and *Death Day*, which chronicled a religious festival and a bullfight. The remaining footage was purchased by another company, which produced a series of "educational shorts," called *Mexican Symphony*. In 1954, after long negotiations, the Museum of Modern Art bought the bulk of the footage and created a series of *Study Films*.

It wasn't until the 1970s that Eisenstein's assistant, Grigori Alexandrov, had the opportunity to edit the remains of the film in the Soviet Union, following Eisenstein's notes and drawings. This version was released as *Que Viva Mexico!* Part documentary, part visionary travelogue, part dramatic epic, the brilliant images and composition in the silent film—narrated in Russian and set to an often overly dramatic score—are a romantic and loving tribute to the evolution of Mexico, from a pre-Columbian paradise to the struggles against the Porfirio Diaz dictatorship, to its revolutionary mix of indigenous and modern ways.

Eisenstein would never see the print of his film. He returned to a volatile Soviet Union, and due to a series of problems would not direct until the late 1930s. While one film would be banned for political reasons, he made two other films, including the celebrated *Alexander Nevsky*, which received the Stalin Prize.

Eisenstein died of a heart attack in 1948, not long after his 50th birthday. While *Que Viva Mexico!* would always remain a tragedy for him, he wrote that he considered his time in Mexico "of highest creative excitement . . . which nourished all subsequent work."

For Sinclair, who would run for governor of California in 1934 and eventually win the Pulitzer Prize for his popular novel, *Dragon Teeth*, his new-found friendship with Sol Lesser was "the best thing that we got out of this whole experience."

The Himalayan Parchment

BARRY LOPEZ

IN THE TWENTY-SIXTH DYAD of the consul Aspect Deese's administration, in the District of Hernia on the northern frontier of Aramea, in old Syria, the Blessed Traveller Carlos Deauville arrowed a man named Mustaf Quail, variously described as a bandit, a sedator, and a krupac thief. The man died, at his forty-first year. What occurred during the encounter, on an otherwise deserted stretch of road between Guh and Pessip, is not in red dispute. Nor is Deauville's cause in Mustaf Quail's death. Only Quail's behaviour in those moments holds us rapt.

Predictably, Deauville has arced self-defence and he so pleaded before a rank of judges in Rusem, the bi-capital of Hernia. Quail's locute advanced banditry, a route as predictable. The duodecimo question of the self and its defence, however, so emergent in lethal encounters in recent years, has occluded the minds of the render judges. Their stymie is now five weeks.

The old argument of action from within the community has been put forth by Deauville's parents, the "white cell defence" of a single human thwarting ordinary evil. The estate of Quail has denied and instead arcs rapacity, the even older argument of blood rise.

It has been two days since I rapided here from Rome, dispatched against the impasse, and I write here in my room outlooking the city after the first day of actuation. I appreciated Quail as a treacherous mist and appreciated Deauville as a clerestory, but this barely prises the drapes on their encounter. Quail, for example, lost his authority in an incident in the Lasek Wars and might have been a mashkanshapir, a person afraid to be kinded.

After plausibles this morning, I retired the pleas and stood recess until I could walk the nine pols to the wreck site and examine the milieu. I paced it fully an hour and then, in the way of esotericos, began an interrogation of the stones by the roadside and, more importantly, of the water table shimmering deep below. Though I am not permitted to render a decision on this basis, I could then backward through such evidence as blood stain pattern and crease in the dust and arrive correctly at a just decision, the sole responsibility of an impasse judge, whatever his skills and methods.

I took the precaution here, in the near village of Jupah, of employing the Weaver's Rite to assess nearness-to-truth in my judgment, and endured an anxious hour while sixteen messianics heebled my story. (They were four-square arranged. I stipulated to each one in turn and then blurted to their fire queries. The fifteen vers to one cryout produced a danis in the second harmony. So, graced on stride, I returned to Rusem.) It remains for me in this room in the hours ahead only to Dress the Birds of Yamat.

From the desk where I write, I can see the cedars of this city in their evening mist of ghost water against an Hispanic blue sky, speckled with docent clouds embrailed across a northwest wind. The clouds are the colour of ripe tamarinds, and the sill of my view is mud-washed arches in the walled neighbourhood of Bess. I respire easily to the tableau.

In my examination early this afternoon of that spot in the road, my colloquy with witness entities, this is the story I received, which has my confidence. Deauville was passing through the vapour of the once-village of Nef, on his way to Guh, when Quail stepped into his way and asked after directions to Ked, a now-village in the same district. Deauville shook his head, no, he was not from here. Quail asked then what district was he sworn to, and Deauville answered to Hujuk, beneath the Carpathians. The conversation went this way (in good render), Quail's words first:

"Ked is my father's village, dormant to me, but calling. I am uncertain to go."

"Your father receives my respect. I am a Blessed Traveller, a water stiller."

"Don't know it."

"After the Trouble, some lakes and the like—giffs, luns—could not stop trembling. I still the water."

"Can you still my blood quaking?"

"Why is that?"

"Krupac thief. A compulsion, after the Lasek Wars."

"No, not my power."

Here the conversation halts. Quail steps back, slaps himself in the face hard three or four times and comes into tears. A moment, then he bites into the knuckles of his left fist. Blood mounts in the punctures, and he holds forth his hand to Deauville to see. The blood vibrates on the crown of the rigid fist, glistening too with tears. Now Deauville:

"I could try."

"I recompense with Mirish and Dank coinage."

"Only food. Food only."

"My pack holds seven quotients of polir leaves. Five?"

"Lay down. Lie here, in imitation of a lake."

"My father thanks you. The community of Ked, my opening, offer their thanks."

Quail stripped his fabrics and lay prone in the sand, sprawled in the shape of a quoin. Now Deauville again, concentrating:

"Once, actually, an aqueduct here."

"Oh yes. I can feel it over us."

The wind rippled the hair on Quail's back, thick above the shoulder blades. From his mouth a prissy sound came, like dog lapping. Deauville dortled around him in incantation and dance for an hour, while the sun struck at them and Quail twisted in the wind whip of his inner blood, lapsed, then writhed again and silented.

And it was done. Quail rose up in water movement and dressed. He took five quotients of polir leaves from his pack, and here is how it began. Now Quail:

"Four to you, Traveller."

"Black, not rightness."

"Put you to drift then, in the once-village of Nef."

"I will ask you to resign your wish, or at the first breath to make attack, you will inhale a Pomerek arrow to its fletchings."

"I will scald you with words."

"I will break your language as glass, and you will speak Caddish all the days of your life left."

"I will insinuate dogs in your spleen."

"I will inflate your lungs with the breath of vultures."

"I will incarcerate your hands."

So it went, in the western Harp style, the men moving in the high-legged prance of Gosic spiders on face-off. They were watching for lull, of course, the break in awareness that would permit Deauville to put the bindleread to sleep, Quail to choke the water stiller from Life. A sharp pain, prosaic as indigestion or serious as a gall stone, I cannot say, gave Deauville half-mind and Quail storted nigh but not quick enough. A smaller arrow, Wafdek rather than Pomerek, pierced the left lung, opened the right ventricle of the heart, and slit the trachea. His caterwaul drowned in gurgle. His knees plunged, he keeled and was dimmed. The Blessed Traveller called to the roadway stones to witness, to the deep table of water and to whisps of volpweed and cadgarsh shrub. He knelt the corners of the grounds and began the Abyssinian Prayer to the Right Dead for the null transport of the soul of the krupac thief.

While the event is clear in its unfolding, its interior remains difficult to tunnel. Strictly viewed, a Blessed Traveller is liable if he does not declare himself in the western Harp style of die-rant. But I regard the thief's knowledge of the cure that the Traveller effected, this demonstration of his power, as exonerating the Traveller on this point. Also, his recital of the Abyssinian Prayer, an act of compassion, further exonerates him because of the certitude of divine intercession here. What wants us, as I have said, is to tone-strike Mustaf Quail. An interior torture deeper than blood quake articulated Quail's reneging, pronged his death. I am staking that Quail was a mashkanshapir, someone whose loss of community standing mangle-inverts. His loss of peer authority in the Lasek Wars was in the arena of his central identity. It caused him to arc from the warrior notion that an act of cruelty was in essence an act of aggression. In my opinion Mustaf Quail was afraid to receive/be kind because he never retrieved his sense of authority. His adolescence redominated, and he became, in the pose of a man, a parasite upon his community, something Carlos Deauville saw and, lethally threatened, felt justified in destroying.

In the popular mind, the self-declared thief is well rid of; but his execution must have a dimension of justice about it or the consequences to anyone befriending the water stiller in the future are dire, subtle but dire. The water stiller requires not justification but the judgment of the community he has so directly served.

My recapture of those moments on the Guh–Pessip road turns on a bit of sleuth: ground water running beneath the once-village of Nef witnesses the daylighted world, and holds in its sprawling and continuous memory everything from the Uyek Assyrian Dynasty to these days of ours. I feel here the sphereness I require to make my shut-case for dismissal of the incident.

Once there were feuds, of the sort that led to holocausts and finally of course to the Trouble, and they could come again. You can see the shadow casting of it in this meeting between a Called and a bolter. I will tick it here, but where else might it occur; and if I may self-lift this little, what if it comes before a judge less adept?

I reconnoiter the sky fully, every pull of colour, every drive of star and planet apparent to my eye, before I arrange, now, to write out my judgment, this time with the quill of a damask heathen of Once Iraq, terse sentences on a parchment of Grun, passed down from the days of Tibet. It crabs and scolds the table as I palm it flat and regard the ink erase of other judgments. I will geometer the design of the self and the compose of the community and etiolate the thief. The night air at my temples stiffens now with the metallic notes of a celesta, and I begin with the image of derelict vegetation, resolute on that desolate stretch of road.

The Princess and the Flying Bee

NATHALIE ROBERTSON

Once upon a time there was, in a world far away, two friends: a Princess and a Flying Bee.

And the Bee landed on a flower,
and the Princess goed another way.

And the Bee sees the Princess was gone. He landed off the flower and he flied into the forest and he saw the Princess turning the other way. And she was turning another corner. She crossed the street and the Bee kept following her, and she was going home.

And when the Princess was home, the Bee was
right after her. And they danced until eight
o'clock. And they woke up the next morning, and they were together.
And they remembered they went through the forest, and when they went
through the forest the Princess was home and the Bee was right after her.

And they danced until dinnertime.

There Is No Word For Home

ISABEL HUGGAN

When day and life draw the horizons
Part of the strangeness is
Knowing the landscape.
   – Margaret Avison, "From a Provincial"

IN THE COUNTRY where I live, there is no word for home. You can express the idea at a slant, but you cannot say *home*. For a long time this disconcerted me, and I kept running up against the lack as if it were a rock in my path, worse than a pothole, worse than nothing. But with time I have habituated myself and can step around it, using variants such as "the hearth" or "the house where I live" when I mean to say home. More often, *chez moi* is the phrase I substitute to indicate not only physical location and the sense of family, but also my comportment, even my point of view. However, if I wish to speak of "going home to Canada," I can say "my country" or "the place of my birth," but I can't say I am going *chez moi* when I am not, for as long as I reside in France—most likely the rest of my life—this is where I will be *chez moi*, making my home in a country and a language not my own. I am both home and not-home, one of those trick syllogisms I must solve by homemaking, at an age when I should have finished with all that bother.

In the foothills of the Cévennes I live in a stone house which was, until only a few decades ago, home to silkworms. Thousands upon thousands of them, squirming in flat reed baskets laid on layered frames along the walls in what was then *la magnanerie*, a place for feeding silkworms, and is now a bedroom. For the duration of their brief lives, these slippery dun-coloured creatures munched mulberry leaves, fattening themselves sufficiently to shed their skins four times before they'd stop eating and attach themselves to twigs or sprigs of heather on racks above the baskets. With a sense of purpose sprung from genetic necessity they'd then spin themselves cocoons, where they'd sleep until they were plucked from their branches and dunked in huge kettles of hot water. Perhaps some luckier ones were allowed to waken and complete the magic of metamorphosis—there must be moths, after all, to furnish next season's eggs—but silk manufacturers preferred the longer filament which comes from whole cocoons. There are sacrifices to be made for beauty, and if the life of a lowly and not very attractive segmented grub must be that sacrifice, perhaps that is the Lord's will.

The Lord's will rests heavy on the high blue hills of the Cévennes, for here God has been imagined in Calvinist clothes, a moral master whose plans for man and beast alike are stern. This little-inhabited part of southern France (the mountainous northern corner of Languedoc, much of which is now a national park) has long been the heart of Protestant resistance to easy and sinful Catholicism: from the mid-1500s, revolt against Paris and the Church continued, with appropriate bloodshed on all sides, until the *Édit de Tolérance* in 1787 allowed those few Huguenots who remained the right to practice their religion.

The rugged terrain, the hidden valleys, and craggy cliffs are geologically appropriate to the Protestant mind; this is country where life is not taken lightly. The harshness of Reform doctrine seems even to show itself in the architecture of Huguenot houses such as mine: angular, stiff-necked houses, tall and narrow and small-windowed against the blasts of winter or the blaze of summer. Nevertheless, graceless and severe though it may appear from the outside, the cool, dark interior of this house is like a blessing when you step in from the painful dazzle of an August day. It is not for nothing that the stone walls are nearly a metre thick or that the floors are laid with smooth clay tiles.

Sometimes I wake in the early morning before it is light, the still, dark hours of contemplation: how have I come to be here? But there is nothing mysterious; the reason is mundane: it is the will not of God but of the Scottish-born man to whom I have been married since 1970. We agreed that when he retired we would settle here, after the first time we came hiking in these mountains nearly a decade ago and he knew he was *chez soi dans les Cévennes*. His experience was profound, affecting him in some deep, atavistic way I would not understand if I had not felt the same inexpressible magnetic, nearly hormonal pull when I first set foot in Tasmania and knew myself to be home.

When it happens, this carnal knowledge of landscape, it is very like falling in love without knowing why: the plunge into desire and longing made all the more intense by being so utterly irrational, inexplicable. The feel of the air, the lay of the land, the colour and shape of the horizon, who

knows? There are places on the planet we belong and they are not necessarily where we are born. If we are lucky—if fate wills it, if the gods are in a good mood—we find them, for whatever length of time is necessary for us to know that yes, we belong to the earth and it to us. Even if we cannot articulate this physical sensation, even if language fails us, we know what home is then, in our very bones.

I say jokingly that I am a WTGW—a whither-thou-goest-wife, an almost extinct species, but one with which I have become familiar in the thirteen years we have lived abroad because of my hus-band's work in development. I have met many other women who have done the same as I: one weighs the choices, and one follows. And so it follows that I shall make this house home and attempt to put down roots, find out how to grow in and be nourished by this rocky foreign soil. I early learn the phrase *je m'enracine ici* as if to convince myself I can really do it. Besides the house, we have a stone barn and a couple of hectares of land—a few olive trees, a small field that will be an orchard someday, part of a hillside and the bank of a stream which separates our land from that of the nearby monastery where Charlemagne is said to have taken mass. No doubt one of those "X slept here" tales, nevertheless the fact that it could possibly be true is enough to cloak the entire area in the rich sauce of history. Why should this make living here more palatable? But it does.

ONE WINTER'S DAY I NOTICED a man with a metal detector in the vineyard along the road, and when I asked what he was looking for, was told "Roman coins." Although he appeared to be a rough sort of fellow—shaggy hair, ruddy face, ill-fitting old clothes, the type you see selling junk at flea markets—he was kindness itself, and took time to give me a pocket version of local history, the ebb and flow of Celts, Greeks, Romans, Goths, Saracens—you name them, they were here, and they left their mark everywhere. He lifted a chunk of rose-brown brick from the soil and gave it to me: "Roman," he said. No more Roman than I am, I thought, but I took it graciously and carried it home, a reminder that everywhere around me there are bits and pieces of the past, visible and invisible. In *Lives of a Cell*, Lewis Thomas said, "We leave traces of ourselves wherever we go, on whatever we touch." Perfume lingering in the air, letters in the attic, the pressure of your hand on the small of my back as we danced, tears on the pillow, a shard of pottery, a piece of brick.

There's a cream-coloured brick above the doorway of our barn on which is carved 1853, the same year a boatload of my poor Scottish forebears settled themselves down on the shores of Lake Huron, thrown off their heathery land for the sake of sheep back home in the Hebrides. Seemed a long time ago, 1853, when I was growing up in Canada: seems yesterday, here. The barn is considered relatively new, and even our house, built a hundred years before that, is not considered *old*: old is reserved for the ruins of the local twelfth century chateau or the romanesque church we can see across the vineyards. Time passes unevenly from place to place, has different weight and value. Here, I think, it seems to have collapsed, folding in and compressing itself into something deep and dense, a richer, thicker brew than I, a child of the New World, am accustomed to. The air I breathe *chez moi* is full of old souls; the noise of the stream falling over the dam is like the sound of distant voices.

Walking in the woods in Canada—the Gatineau, Algonquin Park, the maple bush behind our house—the childish game in my head was always "explorer," playing at discovery, making it seem new; hiking in the Cévennes, there are different games of retrieval, understanding one's place in the context of others. Just a few metres from the path, a ruined stone wall emerges, moss-covered and beautiful, in the midst of forest which, until that moment, seemed like wilderness. There have been so many other people here before me, and the tangible evidence of that raises questions, gives me pause, thrills me to my boots.

WHY SHOULD BITS of brick and stone be so seductive? The people who passed through this land have nothing to do with me: this is not my story.

Nevertheless, I am touched by the past and stand with tears in my eyes reading a plaque at a mountain pass commemorating the deaths of seven local partisans in the Resistance: the heros in the Cévennes are *camisard* and *maquis*, forever resisting. At the corner where I turn to go to market stands a memorial to the destruction of a German convoy in 1944; courage, death, victory, freedom. All the big notions, over and over again, on the same ground.

I spend much time reading books about the region to learn who was here when, and why; I am getting a sense of how things fit together. It is essentially the same activity as my borrowing *Life in the Clearings* from the Public Library when we moved from Toronto to Belleville, Ontario in 1972, endeavouring to know something about the Moodies' stone house I passed on my way to work at the daily newspaper. I felt I was accumulating material that had something to do with my Canadian life, perhaps some vague fantasy of treading in the journalistic footsteps of Susanna herself. Nothing I read will ever help me to fit here. I will always be an outsider, no matter how much history I swallow. But I persist.

Throughout this region, which has been emptied of people for reasons as various as war, famine and financial failure, there are terraced hillsides, where once mulberry trees flourished: although some terraces are used today for growing onions, they are mostly abandoned, mute testimony to change and loss. In the rafters of our barn there are still bunches of old mulberry branches, the leaves dry and brown, left behind after the raising of silk-worms was no longer profitable even as cottage industry. Most silk factories in the Cévennes had already closed by the end of the nineteenth century, but some farmers continued to use the upper part of their houses as *magnaneries* until the 1940s. Measuring time by the remembrance of Yolande, one of five elderly local women who recently came for tea, it seems that was true in mine. Yolande, close to seventy, recalls being in this house as a child—she was born round the corner in the monastery which has long been divided among several local families—and when I took her and the others on a tour of the house to see our renovations, she threw up her hands in astonishment as we entered the bedroom, recalling how it had looked when *la vieille dame Augustine* lived here and kept *les vers à soie.* "*Quelle différence!*" she said, shaking her head in disbelief.

The ladies came to tea with my friend the widow Arlette, as I'd suggested she bring the companions with whom she walks for exercise on Tuesdays. When they arrived at the door they were buzzing with curiosity, as if an electric current were lighting up their lovely old faces: unheard-of in this rural community to be invited in and allowed to look through someone's house. What a grand opportunity! How amazing is this Canadian! I heard in the village the week after that it was said, in tones not of censure but delight: *Elle est très ouverte!*

Arlette Malavel has been very fond of me since two years ago when she met me on the road and told me that over the winter her husband Fleury had died; I burst into tears and we wept together, arms round each other, both of us moved by the other's sadness. He was a lovely man, Fleury, with bright blue eyes, a big white moustache and wine-red cheeks, and he kept a little mill on the river, just the other side of the bridge that leads to our long lane. The mill had turned out whole-grain flour for well over a century, until it was ruined in the dreadful flood of October '95 when what is normally a shallow stream suddenly, overnight, roared swollen and crazy, a raging white-water tor-rent carrying trees and horses and cars in its rushing course. The hors-es are dead and gone but uprooted trunks and rusting fenders still lodge along its banks like mournful memo-ries, reminders that flood and drought are a double scourge in this countryside.

I met the Malavels the first summer we arrived to work on the old house, before we really lived here. Not yet having a telephone was no hardship since there's a public booth by the village school, only a ten-minute walk away. One evening on my way to make a call, I met Arlette on the road, and after the first polite "*Bon soir, Madame*" she struck up a conversation, evidently curious about who in the world I was. Once her questions were an-swered, she offered the use of the telephone in her small apartment in the monastery. A woman in her sixties, with short hair that deep purple-henna shade favoured by so many Frenchwomen, and a sharpness to her features which I recognize now as Cévenol, she insisted I meet Fleury, who was in the monastery gardens, planting beans. I offered to help

and he accepted, after being assured that I knew how: three beans to a hill. As darkness fell upon us and the stars came out and bats joined the swooping martins overhead, we worked up and down the rows, me chatting away in cheerful high-school French, sticking beans in the soil, patting them down, planting them and myself in this place. And now poor Fleury is dead and the mill stays ruined and empty for he never taught his son the trade, and Arlette has given up their sec-tion of the monastery, and lives alone in a nearby hamlet.

Everything, for me, dates from that hour of planting beans. The fa-miliar rhythm, the smell of damp earth, somehow knowing where I was be-cause I was in a garden. The strangeness of know-ing the landscape began then, has continued, goes on. This may not be *home*, but there are moments I startle myself nearly witless because I actually know where I am: know exactly the curve of the road to the village and where to slow down, or when to expect the light in the early afternoon to catch itself in the crystal prism I hung last year in the window, or which way to turn to find Orion's Belt in the clear night sky. Emotional geometry, physical knowledge of the deepest sort, the kind that resides under the skin, beneath history, be-yond words.

DURING THESE YEARS spent outside Canada, I've lived by something I read in an interview with surgeon Chris Giannou: "Home is not a physical, geographic entity. Home is a moral state. The real home is one's friends. I like to think of that as a higher form of social organization than the nation state." With my parents dead and no home to return to (my father's second wife does not allow me in the family house she inherited from my father; my only sister lives in England), this gave me great comfort, especially in our years as expatriates in Kenya or the Philippines, for I figured that even if we were "temporary renters" in those countries, no matter. My real home was somewhere else, invisible but enduring and permanent. I could never be in exile in my heart, in the place where love resides, *chez moi.*

But something in me is changing. I am burrowing down into an actual place now, my hands in the dirt, planting tulip and narcissus bulbs under the wild nettle tree by the barn. It is the feel of the earth I desire, this most primitive need finding expression in an act as simple as digging holes and plunking in bulbs. Has this to do with growing older, approaching the earth itself on new terms? Perhaps. Bent on one knee, I let the leafy humus run through my fingers, thinking: maybe I will be buried here someday. We are told there are already three dead Protestants under the barn, interred two hundred years ago according to local ordinance which allows home burial for non-Catholics. This does not strike me as a particularly morbid thought, but I do not dwell on it long; I am too busy.

Much of my effort has gone toward supervising renovations in the house, getting a bathroom and a kitchen, making the place habitable, cozy. Pictures hung, books on shelves, bouquets of wildflowers on the table. But it is less the house than the surrounding hills to which I attach myself, walking daily and learning to name those wildflowers as I pick them. I am discovering this small truth: to feel "at home" you need to know the proper names for things. Thus I must re-name daisies *marguerites*, call the swallows *hirondelles*, the chestnut tree *chataigner*. It is work, pure and simple. And it is daunting. My mouth cannot produce the liquid sounds required by French, my throat cannot give up a rounded *r*, my tongue cannot do arabesques around the word *heureuse*, my lips purse up to no avail. And worse, my ears. Away from the solitude of my room, I exist in a muddled state of mild incomprehension, seldom sure whether I have properly grasped what has been said: my public stance is one of brave bewilderment, my tone of voice inquiring, apologetic. In some odd way I live at a level beneath language, where words do not touch me—but at the same time as I am trying to "catch on," to understand, to know and be known. In this way I am not myself, at the same time as I am more myself than ever, for there is also constant clear definition. There is no doubt for anyone meeting me that I am not French: *je suis canadienne anglophone.* I will always be foreign, alien, *toujours une étrangère.* A stranger, even *chez moi.*

When I am in Toronto in the summer, sitting in a subway car amused and amazed at the wonderful way the faces of the city have changed since I lived on St. George Street in 1965, I think of how hard it is to learn another language, to get it right, to make yourself fit to the shape of different sounds in your mouth. I want to tell the woman beside me—Cambodian, Peruvian, Ethiopian, Croatian—*I know how you feel. It's not easy. It's lonely and tough. But trust me, start with little things: flowers, trees, birds. Make a little garden, if only in your head. Get to know your neighbours. Dream of home and it will come to you.* But then I think how incredibly presumptuous of me to offer platitudes, and I do not reach out, I stay silent. What can I possibly know of their plight? Why should they care that I, who appear to belong in this city, also know what it's like to be an outsider? What earthly good might it do? What works for me may work for no one else.

Get to know your neighbours. For me, you see, it's easy. Our house is divided in three parts, for in a manner not unlike the Mennonite farmhouses in the part of Ontario where I grew up, the main house extended itself over the years with various outbuildings attached at this side or that. Ours is the central one, and jutting off to one side, rather like the half-stroke of a nearly-crossed *t*, is the section belonging to Dede Domingues, professional comedian. In the summer he and the other two men in his troupe practise their act in his front yard and I sit on my front steps and watch, not getting the jokes but applauding all their slapstick routines. Dede is a small man with big ears and a comic manner: just now, watching him walk to the mailbox, I find myself smiling, for he has the flat-footed gait of a clown.

More importantly, he has something to teach me about appearance and reality. At first, I found myself horrified by his unmowed, untidy and auto-strewn yard, his cement-block outhouse from which the *Mistral* recently blew the tiles off the roof, his utter disregard for bourgeois values: if it is a fine day, he is off on his *vélo*. But Dede is a neighbour without whose generous warmth my life would be barren and dull. He fires the ancient oven attached to our barn and we bake bread and pizza. He fills my bicycle tires with air, he keeps me *au courant* with local gossip, he offers advice and explanation when I am stymied by things bureaucratic, and he'll feed the cat if I'm away. And in autumn he brings me bags of *girolles*, a wild yellow mushroom which, sauteed in butter, tastes like the first time you ever heard Chopin, absolutely extraordinary.

At the rear, there is an addition which would form the top of the *t*, home to the Ennoury family, whose long rambling garden is visible from our terrace on the side nearest the river. Miloud Ennoury is a friendly man but on account of missing teeth his French is sometimes hard to grasp; Zahra, his plump, shy wife, smiles and embraces me each time we meet, but speaks not a word. There are five children, the younger ones still in grade school and the elder three trying to find work. The Ennourys are Moroccan, and they know even better than I what it is to live where you are never completely accepted. We do not talk of this so much as acknowledge it in sideways fashion, discussing the problems of getting jobs as I sit at their round table drinking sweet mint tea or strong black coffee, listening to the frustrations faced by the girls Aiat and Adij and their brother Mahmed. I do what I can to help, typing their resumes, but in a country where unemployment is high and in a region where it's even higher, what colour your skin is and where your parents came from matters more than layout or choice of typeface.

Miloud has worked twenty years in the vineyards of Geneviève Bastide, a middle-aged single woman with a bashful and boyish manner, who always wears a delicate gold chain and Huguenot cross even with her farm clothes, and who owns that section of our house and permits Miloud and his family to live there as part of his salary. Geneviève also keeps goats and in good weather, if she is not occupied tending her vines, can always be found out in the hills with her small herd and her dogs. Aided by her frail old father, she makes and sells small white rounds of goats' cheese from her house on the other side of the village. Often, she has a hard mouldy cheese for sale, which has been kept a very long time in a stoneware jar with herbs. For this, she gives me the following traditional Cévenol recipe: grate the cheese into a bowl and add the same amount of fresh butter and finely chopped walnuts. Mix well and serve on slices of warm baguette. Washed down with ice-cold rosé wine from the local *Cave Coopérative*, the winery where she and Miloud take her grapes every September, this is sustenance of the elemental sort, tasting of this earth, this rain and sun, this air. These people, this place where I live.

DOES THIS SOUND CHARMING, a middle-aged Canadian settling into the rhythms of rural France? I suppose I am seeking to convince myself, and so I choose my words and images to achieve effect, so determined am I to chase ambivalence into the shadows. A line comes into my head; it must be from an old song: *If you can't be with the one you love, then love the one you're with*. Easier said than done, of course—I know all about homesickness, sipping maple syrup from a spoon while listening to a tape cassette of loon calls, endlessly writing letters to friends asking for news, sifting through old photographs, weeping. Yes, I've been there, that strange and dangerous place where longing can blind you to everything else. And so you learn to live with *mal de pays* as with a chronic illness or disability, you salt your days with *nostalgie* … and you compare yourself to the millions of displaced people in the world, refugees who will never see their homes again, and you feel ashamed, and you stop.

You go for a walk in the hills and watch a hawk unwinding on an updraft. You know this hawk; he has a certain territory and he is part of the landscape you now know, as they say, like the back of your hand. Or you put on your gardening gloves, and take your trowel, and another bag of daffodil bulbs, and work hard at making a garden. At night you fall into bed content that you are doing it, you are creating whatever it is that is *chez*. The ghosts of the silkworms are as silent as they were in life and you can sleep without interruption except for the hourly tolling of the bell at the village *Mairie* across the fields. It always rings the hour twice, as if to ensure that its message is heard: Listen, it says.

Pay attention. This is where you are.

This issue is in memory of
Carole Corbeil, 1953-2000

Every day she'd been back from Quebec City, she'd thought about it, thought about going up and watering the plants, but it's been like a tug that she's deliberately ignored.

She didn't want to see it. Didn't want to see the state the little roof garden would be in after weeks of neglect. When it rained yesterday, she was so grateful she almost cried. The skies can look after it, she thought, the skies can do it. I can't go up there. Everything I start ends up a mess. I can't take care of anything.

The late August sun is still hot, but the wind from the lake is cool. Stepping onto the deck, she can smell the fall coming in. She likes that. She is sick of the intensity of summer, she's ready for a new season, even if it pulls the long winter in its wake.

She expected everything to be dead, the earth in the planters to be cracked, the plants hollow, yellow sticks. But the tomatoes, while pale with thirst, have grown way beyond their stakes, and would have fallen over onto the deck if it hadn't been for the morning glory vines that wrapped themselves around them. The morning glories never went up the strands of string she'd stretched onto the trellis. They grabbed the nearest thing, and now their vines are thick and wiry and hardy. The blooms are stretched tight, almost transparent, like china cups full of sky.

—*Voice-over*, Carole Corbeil

THE USUAL SUSPECTS

Tissa Abeysekara is a filmmaker and novelist living in Sri Lanka, where he has written and directed more than fifty documentaries and feature films. His novel, *Bringing Tony Home* was the recipient of the Gratiaen Prize in 1998.

Victor Anant was a poet, novelist, and essay-writer whose journalism appeared in newspapers and magazines throughout the world. Among his books are *The Revolving Man* and *Sacred Crow*. He died in 1999.

Margaret Atwood's most recent novel is *The Blind Assassin*. She lives in Toronto.

Russell Banks is the author, most recently, of the novels *The Sweet Hereafter*, *Rule of the Bone*, and *Cloudsplitter*, and *The Angel on the Roof: New and Selected Stories*.

Jennifer Baichwal is a documentary filmmaker whose films include *The Holier It Gets*, and *Let It Come Down*, on which her piece in this issue is based. She lives and works in Toronto.

John Berger's books include *To the Wedding*, *G.*, and the trilogy *Pig Earth*, *Once in Europa*, and *Lilac and Flag*. He lives in France.

Jeff Biggers is a writer based in Illinois and Italy. He founded the Northern Arizona Book Festival.

Robert Bringhurst's books of poems include *The Beauty of the Weapons* and *The Calling: Selected Poems 1970-1995* . He has studied the Haida language since 1985 and has published several books on Haida art as well as a study of Haida literature, *A Story as Sharp as a Knife: The Classical Haida Mythtellers and Their World* (Douglas & McIntyre / U of Nebraska Press, 1999).

Anne Carson lives in Canada.

Michael Dirda is a writer and senior editor for The *Washington Post Book World*. He is the author of *Readings: Essays and Literary Entertainments*, published this fall by Indiana University Press.

Jeffrey Eugenides is the author of the novel, *The Virgin Suicides*. He is currently a Berlin Prize Fellow at The American Academy in Berlin.

Helen Garner's work includes novels, short stories, journalism and non-fiction. Her most recent books are *The First Stone* (Picador), a best-selling account of a university sexual harassment case, and *True Stories* (Text), her selected journalism. She lives in Melbourne.

Isabel Huggan is the author of two collections of short stories, *The Elizabeth Stories* and *You Never Know*. She left her native Canada in 1987, and is now a resident alien in France.

Michael David Kwan was born in China and has lived in Canada since 1963. He has written two non-fiction books, *Broken Portraits*, and *Things That Must Not Be Forgotten: A Childhood in Wartime China* , which has been shortlisted for the 2000 Kiriyama Pacific Rim Book Prize for Nonfiction. He is also a playwright and screenwriter. He lives and works in Vancouver.

Barry Lopez is a short-story writer and essayist. He is the author of the story trilogy *Desert Notes*, *River Notes*, and *Field Notes*. The short story published in this issue of Brick is from his forthcoming collection, *Light Action in the Carribean*. Lopez lives in Oregon.

Jean Mckay grew up in Vancouver, Calgary and Toronto and now lives in London, Ontario. Her first two books, *Gone to Grass* and *The Dragonfly Fling* were published by Coach House Press, and a new book, *Exploded View*, is coming out from Douglas & MacIntyre in the spring of 2001.

Mary Morris is the author of twelve books — five novels including her most recent *Acts Of God* (PicadorUSA), and three travel memoirs, including *Nothing To Declare: Memoirs Of A Woman Traveling Alone*. Morris teaches writing at Sarah Lawrence College and lives in Brooklyn with her husband and daughter.

Alice Munro is a short-story writer whose most recent collection is *The Love of a Good Woman*. She lives in Ontario.

Walter Murch has been a sound and film editor on numerous films, including *The Conversation*, *The Godfather* movies, and *The English Patient*. He is the author of *In The Blink of an Eye*.

Michael Ondaatje's most recent novel is *Anil's Ghost*. He is a contributing editor to Brick.

Al Purdy is the author of more than twenty collections of poetry and edited a number of Canada's most influential poetry anthologies. He died this year in British Columbia. His collected poems, *Beyond Remembering*, has just been published by Harbour Press.

Jacqueline Rau was born in Strasbourg, France in 1901 and was active in the city's photographic community from the mid-1920s until the beginning of wwii. Although her artistic career resumed briefly after the war, it wasn't until 1988 that her work was rediscovered. In 1991 a restrospective of her work was held in Paris and a book of her photographs, *Jacqueline Rau, Photographies* was published. She died in 1994.

Nathalie Robertson attends daycare and French immersion senior kindergarten. She has travelled extensively in France, Ireland, and British Columbia. Her art may be seen on refrigerators across Canada. Her favourite food is any noodle dish.

Toronto writer and broadcaster **Eleanor Wachtel** is the host of CBC Radio's "Writers & Company" and "The Arts Today". Two selections of her interviews have been published: *Writers & Company* and *More Writers & Company*.

Harold Weber is a Professor of English at the University of Alabama in Tuscaloosa.

OUR THANKS TO:

Gord Robertson for the beautiful new design.

Rick/Simon and Stan Bevington of Coach House Printing.

Esther Hart, Lori Rennie, Sarah MacLachlan, Robert Coover, David Silcox, and Photomethods for a last-minute rescue.

TEXT CREDITS:

The page-turner's sister by Jean Mckay is available from Trout Lily Press, 87 Front St., Stratford, Ont, N5A 4G8.

Michael Dirda's essay is reprinted from *From Readings: Essays and Literary Entertainments* published by Indiana University Press this fall.

Excerpt from *Things That Must Not Be Forgotten: A Childhood in Wartime China* by Michael David Kwan is reprinted by permission of the publisher, Macfarlane Walter & Ross.

"The Sealion Hunter," is reprinted from *Nine Visits to the Mythworld*, courtesy of Robert Bringhurst and Douglas & McIntyre.

Michael Ondaatje's remembrance of Al Purdy will appear in *Beyond Remembering: The Collected Poems of Al Purdy*, being published this fall by Harbour Publishing.

The lines by Faiz Ahmed Faiz in John Berger's remembrance of Victor Anant are drawn from Faiz's book *The True Subject*, translated by Naomi Lazard.

Anne Carson's essay originally appeared in *Brick* no. 53, fall 1996.

Michael Ondaatje's Lost Classic will appear in *Lost Classics*, being published this fall by Knopf Canada.

The Akiro Kurosawa excerpt is drawn from his book *Notes on Filmmaking*. Our thanks to the publisher.

Barry Lopez's story is from his forthcoming collection, *Light Action in the Carribean*, being published this fall by Knopf.

PHOTO CREDITS:

The Jacqueline Rau photos in this issue (pages 2, 58, 83, 93, and 125) are courtesy of the Musée d'Art Moderne et Contemporain de Strasbourg / Cabinet d'Art Graphique / Photographies. Our thanks to Christine Speroni, Sylvain Morand, and Marta Braun.

The dog photos in this issue (pages 7, 62, and 91) are reprinted from *Prince and Others, 1850-1940*, published by Bloomsbury. Our thanks to the publisher and Libby Hall, who collected the photographs.

The illustrations on pages 17, 37, 40, 49, 52, and 166 are by David Bolduc

Page 8: Photo by Paul Bowles

Page 8: Photo by Jane Bowles

Page 15: Photo by Terence Spencer

Page 19: Photo by Bill Belli

Page 26: Photo by Brookie Maxwell, courtesy Vintage Contemporaries

Page 30 and 35: Photos by Chaminda Priyanjith Upasena

ASK AN EDITOR

A continuing public service from *Brick*

Q: *As a member of the general reading public, I admit I have next to no idea of what goes on between writer and editor in the corridors of the literary-magazine establishment. Will you enlighten me?*

A: This is a question we here at *Brick* get all the time. Instead of putting our benighted questioner to sleep with a lengthy atomization of a complicated process, we herewith offer one of the fruits of our recent correspondences. An author writes:

> Here is the next installment of my essay. I have reduced the manuscript by about twenty-five per cent. I have eliminated most of the topics not directly related to my wife. Those eliminated are: the burglary, the disease, vegetables on the roadway, my malaria, my gonorrhea, the skunk, slander, the driver ants, the swearing-in ceremony, my Twi lessons, my speeding problem, my driving test, and the skin lightener.

Such negotiations are but part of the intricate congresses between writer and editor. There are also such considerations as margins and nib size, but we shall return to these topics at another juncture.

AND COMING SOON ...
Lost Classics: the book!
This fall in Canada from Knopf Canada
and next spring in the US from Anchor Books.
Available in fine bookstores everywhere.

THE PARIS REVIEW

Ernest Hemingway   E.M. Forster   Vladimir Nabokov
Norman Mailer   Allen Ginsberg   Italo Calvino   T.S. Eliot
Rick Bass   Dorothy Parker   John Updike   James Merrill
William Faulkner   Elizabeth Bishop   Tennessee Williams
Robert Bly   Lillian Hellman   T.C. Boyle   Sam Shepard
Anne Sexton   James Baldwin   Arthur Miller   Don DeLillo
Harold Bloom   Robert Hass   Neil Simon   P.L. Travers
Thornton Wilder   Jeffrey Eugenides   William Styron
Shelby Foote   Jean Cocteau   William Carlos Williams
Geoffrey Hill   Stephen King   Martin McDonagh
John Dos Passos   William S. Burroughs
Philip Roth   Rebecca West   Mark Strand   Woody Allen
John le Carré   Frank O'Hara   Gabriel García Márquez
Wendy Wasserstein   E.L. Doctorow   Margaret Atwood
Eugène Ionesco   Ezra Pound   Toni Morrison   Iris Murdoch
Raymond Carver   John Hollander   Alain Robbe-Grillet
Philip Larkin   August Wilson   V.S. Naipaul   José Saramago
John Ashbery   Terry Southern   Günter Grass   Martin Amis
Milan Kundera   Joan Didion   Jack Kerouac   Octavio Paz
Donald Hall   Tom Wolfe   Peter Matthiessen   John Guare
Marianne Moore   Ken Kesey   John Irving   Kurt Vonnegut
Pablo Neruda   John Cheever   Tom Stoppard   Jim Carroll
David Mamet   W.H. Auden   Harold Pinter   A.R. Ammons
Judy Budnitz   Denis Johnson   Anne Carson   Rick Moody

SINCE 1953

www.parisreview.com - 718.539.7085 - distributed by Eastern News